Timid No More

How I Broke Out of My Comfort Zone by Doing 101 Things and How You Can Break Out of Yours

By Marcy Light

Text copyright © 2013 Marcy Light; updated in February, 2014 after completing all 101 challenges

All Rights Reserved

ISBN-13: 978-1497314986

To my husband Randy and my boys David and Daniel for their love, encouragement, and patience

Table of Contents

1. Milk a cow
2. Do 50 consecutive push-ups
3. Say yes to everything for a whole day
4. Shoot a gun
5. Attend a UU church meeting
6. Go to a roller derby
7. Sing karaoke in a bar
8. Take a trapeze class
9. Make homemade pasta
10. Document a month of my life in photographs
11. Learn to juggle three balls
12. Climb a tree and take a picture of the view
13. Listen to 10 classic albums all the way through
14. Watch all of IMDb's Top 250 Movies
15. Make vegan cake pops
16. Attend a New Year's celebration; kiss at midnight
17. Try Zumba
18. Go snowboarding
19. Ride a mechanical bull
20. Give a sample from my gut (replacement task for giving blood)
21. Make eggplant lasagna
22. Complete a spontaneous challenge
23. Eat Pizza at Pepe's
24. Comment on 50 random blogs
25. Influence a person to make a Day Zero list
26. Make a soufflé
27. Memorize a favorite poem
28. Visit a UNESCO World Heritage Site
29. Bake bread from scratch again
30. Travel alone at least overnight
31. Record a song with me playing a bodhrán with my family
32. Walk 10,000 steps a day for an average of six days a week
33. Paint the garage doors
34. Take an art class
35. Volunteer at a soup kitchen or homeless shelter
36. Watch the sunrise and sunset in the same day
37. Try to grow tomatoes again
38. Don't complain about anything for a week
39. Go to Greece
40. Send a secret to PostSecret
41. Read Anna Karenina
42. Have a Philly cheesesteak in Philly
43. Try at least five new recipes while eating vegetarian for a week

44. Relearn "Greensleeves" on the guitar
45. Have dinner by candlelight
46. Declutter my house
47. Jump off a cliff
48. Attend a wine tasting
49. Try at least five savory oatmeal recipes
50. Take a yoga class again
51. Tour a Connecticut brewery
52. Go strawberry picking again
53. Eat meatless at least one day a week on average
54. Brew my own beer
55. Play, give away, or throw out each of the 32 board games in my basement
56. Make cheese fondue
57. Hike Mount Katahdin
58. Go zorbing
59. Make a wooden frame for the old homemade door panels my dad had made
60. Get a pedicure
61. Have my kids pick five ingredients from the grocery store; feature them in a meal
62. Drive a go kart again
63. Go snowshoeing
64. Try a new cuisine
65. Get a makeover
66. Write a haiku each day for a week that sums up or reflects upon the day
67. Go to at least five offbeat or small museums
68. Get a graphic that represents my blog, "(Don't Be) Too Timid and Squeamish"
69. Visit at least three "Road Food" places I have never been to
70. Eat haggis
71. Try to grow sunflowers again
72. Go through the basement bins and donate, sell, or throw out what I can
73. Knit something
74. Make butter
75. Read at least 15 classics I've never read
76. Eat a cheeseburger at Louis' Lunch
77. Make my own hummus
78. Finalize my will
79. Dance my way through Dance Central with Kinect
80. Complete at least one other athletic challenge
81. Cook something with tofu or tempeh
82. Visit at least five "Roadside America" attractions
83. Have a cookout again
84. Make my own nut butter
85. Hit a bucket of golf balls again
86. Go tubing down the Farmington River with my kids
87. Make a fire in the fireplace

88. Give away or throw out the collection of stained glass pieces and scraps in the basement
89. Adopt a word at savethewords.org
90. Clean up something outdoors
91. Go to a farmer's market
92. Make Spambalaya Jambalaya
93. Go to the beach again
94. Eat French fries topped with sweet mango chutney mayo
95. Fast for one day of Ramadan
96. See at least five live shows
97. Make another Shutterfly book
98. Sell some more Elks pins on eBay
99. Give up caffeine for a day
100. Have another oyster pan roast at Grand Central Oyster Bar
101. Complete a video game challenge set by my kids
On completing 101 things in 1001 days

Introduction

> *"Don't be too timid and squeamish about your actions. All life is an experiment. The more experiments you make the better."*
> — Ralph Waldo Emerson

    I hit middle age and realized I routinely turned down new opportunities. When had I become so closed off to adventure? When had I begun to prefer doing nothing to making an effort to get something done or have some fun?

    Over the years, I had become too timid, too squeamish, and, let's face it, too lazy to get out there and try new things. The comforting cocoon I had weaved around my naturally introverted self had become a straitjacket.

    I needed to make a bold move.

    I made a long list of challenges to tackle. Some scared me. Some I knew I would enjoy, but I never seemed to get around to doing. And some I was just too lazy to ever get around to doing.

    I chose serious tasks (stop complaining) and silly tasks (ride a mechanical bull), intimidating tasks (travel alone) and nostalgic tasks (listen to old records).

    Following an Internet meme (see dayzeroproject.com), I made a list of 101 things to do in 1001 days.

    Having to complete a new challenge every 10 days to stay on schedule, I found myself changing, becoming less timid and more assertive, becoming less squeamish and more easy-going.

    My life changed in ways I could never have imagined. I became more active, strengthened my connections with the people in my life, and met new people. And, yeah, I got a lot done and had a lot of fun.

    In this book, I'll share my challenges and give you ideas for challenges you can try.

    Break out of your comfort zone by making your own list. Share your list or your experiences with me in the comments on my blog (http://www.tootimidandsqueamish.com/). You can even send me a handmade postcard to celebrate your courage. I would love to hear from you.

1. Milk a cow

Why you should try it:
Milking a cow by hand is one of those things that we suburban or city folk are ignorant about. Get your hands on an udder stat.

Give it your twist:
- Milk a goat.
- Plant a garden.
- Harvest a chicken.

My experience:
"Well, did you ever milk a cow?
I had the chance one day, but I was all dressed up for Sunday."
– "We Can Talk," The Band

We all gathered round the cow and brushed her, to relax her and help her drop down her milk. She had just been given a bucket full of apples, so she was already in the moo-d, and she was used to fumbling beginners who didn't know their way around a teat.

Perched on my little three-legged stool, I leaned in, trying to see just what was going on down there. Debra, who was leading the workshop on taking care of a family cow, showed me how to milk her. I encircled a teat at the top with my thumb and index finger, held it firmly for a moment to trap in the milk, and squeezed. I was surprised how easily the milk streamed out, as I had imagined some rigorous tugging would be needed. It was like squeezing Go-

Gurt out of a tube, if the tube were an animal's organ and the yogurt were warm milk. I felt the teat instantly refill with milk, ready for another squeeze.

I even had the opportunity to squirt some raw milk straight from the teat into my mouth. I didn't know what to expect it to taste like, but it tasted exactly like milk, of course, warm milk that your mamma would prepare for you if you couldn't get back to sleep after a bad dream.

I spent time in the field with the cows as they chomped up grass as quickly as they could. They effortlessly moved away from my bumbling attempts to pet them. I did get one of the girls to stay near me as I scratched under her neck, though.

Once Pumpkin was milked, Debra took the bucket into another barn to show us how to prepare yogurt, cheese, butter, and ice cream with it.

Debra had a big bucket of milk from the day before, and we ladled off the rich cream from the thin skim milk. The cream always rises to the top, you know.

As Debra churned away at the ice cream, she told us a delightful story about a smoked cheese she had made based on an elaborate recipe from India, where a cow rescue organization nurses injured free-roaming cows back to health. To make the cheese, they follow rituals to collect their milk and dung. They make flattened balls of the dung that are then dried out and filled with ghee (clarified butter) made from their milk. They smoke the cheese with the ghee-filled dung disks in the oven. Debra followed the process as well as she could in northwestern Connecticut and proudly served us the cheese. It was good, with no hint of dung in its flavor.

We took turns churning the butter and the ice cream, and we were able to try both as part of a potluck lunch we shared. (Debra used store-bought pasteurized cream for sharing with us due to some legalities. She clearly took great pride in her grass-fed cows' milk, though, and the butter made from it was a rich yellow.)

This was a lovely way to spend a morning on the farm.

Enjoyment:	8/10
Difficulty:	3/10
Would I do it again?	Sure, if I had the chance.

2. Do 50 consecutive push-ups

Why you should try it:
Setting a specific athletic goal gives motivation and focus to your efforts to get in shape, and the push-up can be done anywhere for free and work several parts of your body at once.

Give it your twist:
(Check with a medical professional before beginning any fitness program.)
- Planks
- Sit-ups
- Pull-ups

My experience:
Victory! I had been slogging away at the dreaded push-up for over six months. I'd sure had my ups and downs. (Groan.)

Over the course of several months, I settled into a routine that worked well. This was a typical workout, which was based on the "Week 5, Day 3" workout in the 100 push-ups plan. I modified it by taking a longer break between sets.
- Warm up by walking on the treadmill for five minutes
- First set – 18 push-ups; treadmill for .25 miles
- Second set – 18 push-ups; treadmill for .25 miles
- Third set – 20 push-ups; treadmill for .25 miles
- Fourth set – 20 push-ups; treadmill for .25 miles
- Fifth set – 17 push-ups; treadmill for .25 miles

- Sixth set – 17 push-ups; treadmill for .25 miles
- Seventh set – 20 push-ups; treadmill for .25 miles
- Eighth set – maximum number of push-ups, at least 45, which I never quite manage consecutively at the end of a workout. I break it up as needed.

So in about 45 minutes, I walk two miles toward my 10,000 steps a day, do *175 push-ups*, and watch a TV show to boot.

A little *mental trick* really helped when I tried to complete more than 20 at a time. I used to count by fives in my head — 5, pause, 10, pause, 15, pause, 20, pause… and something like 30 seemed insurmountable. The trick was to start thinking of them in sets of 20, so I would do 20, and then start a new set of 20. So 40 just became 20 plus 20, and 50 became 20 plus 20 plus another 20 that I didn't have to finish. I guess it sounds silly, but it really made a difference.

Like I said, I worked on this goal for over six months. (The program is designed to take six weeks. What?) I was so relieved to reach it! I spent several months seriously doubting I could ever do it.

Now, nobody tell me to try to do 100!

Thinking of taking on a push-ups challenge? Some tips:

- **Be safe**. Check with a medical professional before beginning any new fitness routine.
- **Be patient**. A lot of people start and then give up when the increased numbers get too difficult. Repeat the workouts as often as you need to until you are ready to move on and increase your numbers.
- **Think in sets**. When you get into higher numbers, think of them as sets of a certain number, rather than as one at a time. (See the "mental trick" above.)
- **Do the workouts consistently**. Like Woody Allen said, "Eighty percent of success is showing up." Put in the workouts, and you will make progress. If you are really tempted to skip a workout, at least do a certain small number of push-ups. You may find that you are willing to continue after getting over that first hurdle. For me, the first set was always one of the hardest. (Of course, if you have any pain that may be an injury, stop and get it checked out.)
- **Track your progress**. Record your workouts using an online push-ups logger or a simple chart. Seeing progress over time is very motivating.
- **Take rest days**. Do the workouts three days a week.
- **Add other exercises**. My Cardio Tennis instructor is fond of saying that three basic exercises can give people an all-around workout: push-ups, crunches, and lunges.

Enjoyment: 1/10
Difficulty: 9/10
Would I do it again? No, but I'd like to be able to do 20 at a time.

3. Say yes to everything for a whole day

Why you should try it:
It's fun to open yourself up to whatever new experiences may come along.

Give it your twist:
- Do your partner's chores for a week.
- Agree to go to a random movie.
- Attend a workshop on someone else's favorite hobby.

My experience:
As I secretly started my "Say yes to everything" day, I imagined scenes from the Jim Carrey movie *Yes Man*:

Learn Korean? *Yes*. Get in a fight? *Let's go!* Ride a motorcycle? *You bet*. Get a mail-order bride? *Why not?*

Instead, my day plodded along with nobody asking me to do much of anything:

Can I have $10? *OK*. Can I get on your computer? *Yep*. Could you put this in the recycling? *Umm-hmmm*.

Then I met my friend Joy for a walk. This was risky, I knew. Joy and I have been friends since we met at Tae Kwon Do lessons years ago, and we usually get together for something fitness related: hiking, walking, a few 5Ks together.

After my last 5K, the Rugged Maniac, I decided it was time to retire; I walk every day, but I have never, ever liked running. Joy had been asking me recently to join her in a couple of 5Ks, and I had finally let her know that I had called it quits on the running.

I Know What's Coming

And then, as we walked along a chilly linear trail, our talk turned to an upcoming event.

In my head, I pleaded: "Don't ask it, Joy. I've already turned you down."

"The Fitathlon looks really fun. No mud, no water. Just clean obstacles," Joy said.

"Oh yeah?" I tried to sound as uninterested as possible.

"It's in April. You'll need to get ready for hiking in Peru." She knew I was worried about the Inca Trail. She's clever, this one.

"I know," I muttered, staring straight ahead.

"What are you doing to get ready?"

"It's not until August," I said.

"You have to start getting ready! You'll need a good six months."

I knew what was coming. I would have to say yes. "Oh, I'll get ready," I assured her. "I'll do some hiking and whatnot."

"Do you want to do the Fitathlon with me?"

And there it was. Like Brett Favre and Michael Jordan before me, I would be coming out of retirement one last time.

Failed attempts

Just like with my "Don't complain about anything" challenge, this one took me several tries to complete. I am a teacher, and I failed on two different school days as I reflexively spat out about 15 no's before I remembered to say yes:

Can I use my notes on the quiz? *No.* Can I get a drink? *Not now.* Can I go to the bathroom? *You just got here late from lunch!*

I guess I got off easy. My husband had recently been making random, weird requests. (Not like that, people.) A few days earlier I was experimenting in the kitchen and made homemade caramel sauce (divine). I gleefully told him how good it was and that I had picked up cookies and cream ice cream. He complained that I should have gotten vanilla.

"Don't worry, honey. It's gonna be so good."

"No, caramel has to have vanilla," he said.

I reached Level Indignant in a flash. "Are you seriously complaining when we have ice cream and *homemade* caramel sauce?"

"Would you run out and get vanilla?" he said.

"I can't believe you would expect me to–"

He couldn't keep from laughing. "I was just testing if it was your 'Say yes to everything' day. You're so easy."

Enjoyment:	3/10
Difficulty:	6/10
Would I do it again?	No, I'm relieved it wasn't worse.

4. Shoot a gun

Why you should try it:
Get a basic understanding of gun safety.
Give it your twist:
- Go skeet shooting.
- Try archery.
- Hit a target with a BB gun.

My experience:
As a kid, I was steeped in a broth of James Bond, with a heavy dose of Dirty Harry mixed in. I also have a weirdly defective startle impulse and routinely scream during benign situations if I am surprised. People think I'm kidding, but I really can't control it.

So it was with a mix of excitement and dread that I headed to the shooting range to fire a handgun for the first time. I got a safety lesson first from Jordan, a friend of my husband's whose Baer 1911 .45 I would be firing.

The .45 is a big gun. I was scared and let out a yelp from the big kick during my first few shots. I was surprised how quickly I got used to it, though. I started by loading just one round at a time so that I wouldn't have live ammunition in the gun during the kick.

Once I settled in, I fired three rounds in succession, since that is a better method for shooting at zombies, my target of choice.

I stayed alert and cautious throughout our session. A man a few lanes away was firing a cannon that I felt through my feet every time he shot. It's hard to relax around that, but I did get more comfortable.

The three of us only fired about 50 rounds, to the surprise of the man at the desk. Once I finished, I was itching to get out of there quickly, feeling like I didn't want to press my luck.

I took care of Zombie Becky, but Zombie Roxie may be coming for me in my nightmares tonight.

Enjoyment: 7/10
Difficulty: 6/10
Would I do it again? Yes.

See video and more photos:
http://www.tootimidandsqueamish.com/2011/05/die-zombie-becky/

5. Attend a UU church meeting

Why you should try it:
Explore your spirituality. Your beliefs may have changed.

Give it your twist:
- Visit a Buddhist temple.
- Go to a sweat lodge.
- Read a book about a different faith.

My experience:
As someone who has lost her religion, I still seek the community that a church can provide. Over the past few years, I have occasionally attended church services, but I've been an imposter.

I was curious to attend a church service where I could feel at home. The Unitarian Universalist church, while based upon a legacy of Judeo-Christian beliefs, doesn't emphasize belief in a certain creed.

I felt welcome and enjoyed all the accoutrements of a church visit that I usually enjoy — flowers, candles, music — as well as the message I usually enjoy — love, compassion, justice — without the aspects that unfortunately can come along with organized religion — intolerance, judgment, superstition — not to mention all that kneeling every couple of minutes.

During the UU service, the happy, supportive atmosphere was enhanced by hand clapping to a crowd-pleasing, secular song:

"Lean on me, when you're not strong
And I'll be your friend
I'll help you carry on

For it won't be long
'Til I'm gonna need
Somebody to lean on"
– "Lean On Me," Bill Withers

The lyrics fit perfectly with what I long for from religion, the sense of a community of people who care for and support each other.

While the minister delivered her welcoming message, I reflected on my tangled religious history. I was raised a Catholic, but for most of my life, my thoughts on religion have been rife with uncertainty, summed up by a scene from an old Woody Allen movie: "How the hell do I know why there were Nazis? I don't know how the can opener works!"

During the last decade or so, though, I have moved from the uncertainty that placed me in the agnostic camp over to that other "A" word, atheism, which is treated as a dirty word in America.

I don't advertise it, but if people ask me my beliefs, I tell them. They sometimes will whisper, "Yeah, I don't believe either," like we've admitted something shameful.

History, though, is full of shame, centuries of outrageous horror caused by organized religion. And when something like the Newtown school shooting happens and someone like Mike Huckabee says it happened because God has been removed from public schools, that's where some more shame belongs. What must people around the world think of my country when they hear these idiots? I know in my heart that if there were a God, even he could never love a person like that, let alone create him.

Despite my lack of belief, I love the world's religions the way I love any good story. The ancient Greeks couldn't understand the science behind the crops withering and dying each winter. They imagined their harvest goddess, Demeter, in the depths of despair at her innocent daughter Persephone taken away by the god of the underworld. I picture an ancient Greek mother trying to come up with an explanation for why the seasons change. She couldn't, of course, any more than she could explain the death of a child. So Demeter mourned while Persephone sat with Hades on the throne.

A great story. I just don't believe in it.

Toward the end of the UU service, the minister shared a thought-provoking sermon about pity being the near enemy of compassion. It was inspired by a mystery novel, *The Cruelest Month*, which had been the reading earlier in the service. I enjoyed the sermon, and I felt relief that I didn't have to pretend to believe in stories that I don't think are true.

For those of you who find comfort in your faith, I sometimes envy you and wish I still believed, but I also wish that we could grow beyond religion. Let's face our fears of the unknown, and let's make this life worth living.

Now if only I could understand how the can opener works.

Enjoyment:	5/10
Difficulty:	3/10
Would I do it again?	Yes.

6. Go to a roller derby

Why you should try it:
These women are skating their hearts out for your entertainment.

Give it your twist:
- See an NHL game.
- Go ice skating.
- Learn to rollerblade.

My experience:
The Queen City Cherry Bombs defeated the Yankee Brutals in the opening match of the CT RollerGirls season in a fast-paced, exciting match.

Enjoyment: 6/10
Difficulty: 1/10
Would I do it again? Maybe.

7. Sing karaoke in a bar

Why you should try it:
If you can humble yourself before a crowd, you can gain confidence to take on other challenges in your life.

Give it your twist:
- Play Laser Tag.
- Perform in a play.
- Tell jokes at an open mic night.

My experience:
I selected "Midnight Rider" by the Allman Brothers Band to sing karaoke, a song I love that also seemed fitting for the setting, the Winchester Café. Nervous enough, I freaked out more when "Midnight Rambler" began to play, a great song, too, but not what I was prepared for. The karaoke man switched it to "Midnight Rider," but it was a slower version by Waylon Jennings. It was all good, though, a lot of fun, and the crowd was very supportive. (I cannot sing!) Group versions of "Gimme Three Steps" and "Girls Just Want to Have Fun" followed.

The most fun moment, though, was on an instrumental break during my debut when I said, "How's everybody doing out there tonight?"

The crowd went wild.

Enjoyment: 8/10
Difficulty: 9/10
Would I do it again? How many cocktails have I had?

8. Take a trapeze class

Why you should try it:
This class was thrilling, and the step-by-step directions made it easier to follow than I would have thought (for people a little more coordinated than I am, at least).

Give it your twist:
- Take a fire breathing class.
- See Cirque du Soleil.
- Walk on hot coals.

My experience:
"Advice from a veteran trapeze performer: Throw your heart over the bars and your body will follow."
— Unknown

Harness on, I looked out from the rooftop trapeze school toward Manhattan's Freedom Tower and gave a half-hearted acknowledgment when my group was asked if anyone was afraid of heights.

Was I still? I'd gone ziplining, rappelling, cliff jumping. I'd arrived an hour early and watched the end of the previous trapeze class, and I was secretly thinking, "Yeah, I got this."

Then I was faced with the ladder. I climbed it as a three-year-old climbs the stairs. Left foot up, rest with legs together. Left foot up, rest with legs together. The ladder swayed back and forth, and my confidence swayed with it. I started in on the internal monologue: "I wanna go back down. I'm so stupid. Why do I get myself into these situations? Oh yeah, my list."

I made it to the top and got even more scared when the ladder ran out. I awkwardly crawled onto the board on my knees. The instructor on top only glanced at me for half a second before stating the obvious: "You're nervous, huh?"

She unhooked me from the ladder safety line and hooked me into the trapeze safety lines.

My heart pounded, and, for this part, my memories take on a cottony, sluggish quality. Did I place my ten toes over the board, legs shoulder width apart, as I had just practiced down below? I evidently had.

The scariest bit was still to come.

Holding onto a ladder with my left hand, I had to lean into the abyss, hips and chest forward, and reach as far as I could to grab a metal bar — the trapeze — with my right hand. It was surprisingly heavy and tried to pull me off the platform.

The instructor held me from behind, so I wouldn't go over until ready, and even if I did, I was hooked into two safety lines with a safety net below. I felt completely sure of my safety, and yet, the fear, the instinctual certainty that I should not be thrusting my hips forward over a drop... You can't argue with that.

I did it, though.

I stepped off, what technically should have been a small jump, and swung forward, flying on a trapeze. I bungled my attempt to hook my legs over the bar, as several of the beginners did, and before I knew it I had followed the command to let go and sit down, down, down into the safety net. Breathing hard, I crawled over to the edge and somersaulted off the net onto solid footing once again.

The instructor gave me some tips, the most basic of which was "breathe." I hadn't realized I had been holding my breath the whole time.

I never did master the tricks, but I climbed that ladder again, leg over leg, and stepped into the abyss with hips forward, breathing, and thinking, "Yeah, I got this."

And then I was free to spend the rest of the day in Manhattan with my husband, exhausted from adrenaline, and glad that the fun was over so that I could relax and enjoy myself.

Enjoyment: 6/10
Difficulty: 9/10
Would I do it again? Yes, I'd like to take another crack at it.

See video and more photos:
http://www.tootimidandsqueamish.com/2013/07/confronting-the-abyss-at-trapeze-school-new-york/

9. Make homemade pasta

Why you should try it:
The ingredients for making your own pasta are probably in your kitchen right now. It's easy.

Give it your twist:
- Make your own gnocchi.
- Cook potato pancakes.
- Bake a homemade lasagna.

My experience:
These are the steps I followed to make homemade whole wheat pasta with fresh tomato basil sauce.

Gather your ingredients for making whole wheat pasta: 1 cup whole wheat flour, 2 eggs (use local farm eggs if possible), pinch salt, water.

Make a well in the center of the flour for the eggs. Mix the eggs into the flour, adding water a tablespoon at a time until a soft dough forms. I used about 5 or 6 tablespoons of water. The dough ball will be a big, sticky mess at first, but keep working it until it comes together. If you add too much water, you can add a little extra flour. Knead it until a nice, elastic dough ball forms.

Let the dough rest for about 10 minutes.

Dust the dough ball, rolling pin, and cutting board surface or counter with flour.

Roll the dough out into a thin sheet. (Mine should have been thinner!)

Roll up the sheet of pasta like rolling up a map, and cut it into thin strips.

Uncurl the cut pasta. You can let this dry if you wish.

Gather your ingredients for the sauce. I made a very simple and quick sauce so that I could highlight the fresh pasta. Fresh tomato and basil sauce: 1 tomato, handful fresh basil, 1 large clove garlic, 2 T olive oil, 2 T parmesan cheese, salt and pepper to taste.

Mince the garlic. Dice the tomato. Julienne the basil.

Sauté the garlic in olive oil on low heat for a few minutes. Add the tomato and cook for a few minutes. Turn off the heat and mix in the basil. Add salt and pepper to taste.

Cook the fresh pasta until al dente. The time will vary depending on whether or not you dried the pasta. It will float to the top when done. Mine took about 3 minutes.

Drain the pasta and toss it with the sauce. Top it with the Parmesan cheese. Add salt and pepper to taste.

Enjoy!

Enjoyment:	6/10
Difficulty:	6/10
Would I do it again?	Maybe.

10. Document a month of my life in photographs

Why you should try it:
Taking pictures throughout my day for a month made me more aware of all the little things going on.

Give it your twist:
- Scrapbook your life for a month.
- Keep a journal each day for a month.
- Write a poem each day for a month.

My experience:
My sons are on the brink of manhood, which makes the mundane bits and pieces of our lives – an egg sandwich prepared for Father's Day, an Impressionist painting for a school project, a new account for a very first paycheck — all the more poignant.

Seeing my rapid-fire photos of June all mixed together reminds me of the wisdom of the great Ferris Bueller, who said: "Life moves pretty fast. You don't stop and look around once in a while, you could miss it."

I featured the photos in a two-minute video, which showed that June was heavy on tennis and social gatherings, exactly how June should be.

It was fun documenting my daily life for a month, but I will be glad not to feel compelled to pull out my phone and say things like, "Let me take a picture of you with your library book" or "Take a picture of me holding the potato salad." My kids will be glad too.

Enjoyment: 5/10
Difficulty: 7/10
Would I do it again? No, it got annoying.

See the video: http://www.tootimidandsqueamish.com/2013/06/a-month-in-the-life-300-photos-in-2-minutes/

11. Learn to juggle three balls

Why you should try it:
It's fun, and you'll get better with practice.
Give it your twist:
- Learn to jump rope double Dutch.
- Dance the Macarena.
- Get good at catching a Frisbee.

My experience:
We all have a lot to juggle. Kids, work, home, exercise, chores ... The list goes on and on.

How do we keep all the balls in the air?

Sometimes we can't quite manage.... Sometimes we can.

And sometimes we need a little help from our friends....

Learning to juggle, even at my beginner status, was very satisfying. I am hopelessly uncoordinated, and it really seemed like I wasn't going to be able to get the hang of juggling at all. (It's as if there's some force working to pull the balls down out of the air).

As my list has been teaching me time and time again, though, if I just stick with something long enough and persevere, I will be successful.

I know juggling is just a silly task, but I am getting inspired to take on more difficult and meaningful challenges.

I just don't know what they are yet.

Enjoyment: 4/10
Difficulty: 9/10
Would I do it again? Yes, I'd like to keep practicing.

See the video: http://www.tootimidandsqueamish.com/2013/11/bar-juggling-scene/

12. Climb a tree and take a picture of the view

Why you should try it:
Who needs a playground? Adventure is right in your backyard.

Give it your twist:
- Try parkour.
- Tackle the monkey bars.
- Complete three chin-ups.

My experience:
A week earlier, my husband had dragged a ladder out to the backyard for me and stood by to take a picture of my second attempt to climb a tree (even though I had already declared this task completed months earlier. I decided that one didn't count, though. It's not easy being me, people, and I never claimed that it was).

And I failed again.

I had flashed him a scared look as I approached the ladder, but I still believed I could do it. I got to the limb I was on last time, stood up, and froze, heart pounding again. My husband had warned me the tree was wet from the rain, but when I was feeling confident, I completely disregarded it, and now in the grip of my fear, I whined, "It's slippery."

I climbed back down, dirty and disappointed.

Climb a tree, take three: I'll take it

At a friend's house, I complained about my nagging worry that I had sullied my pristine list by not really climbing a tree. We were drinking a glass of wine before going out to dinner, and my friends sprung into action. They found me a suitable tree and a jacket to put over my sweater, and they sent me up on my way. I think the wine helped.

Enjoyment: 2/10
Difficulty: 9/10
Would I do it again? No, that one's checked off for good.

13. Listen to 10 classic albums all the way through

Why you should try it:
Why is it that we can get so far away from the joys of our youth? Make an effort to do something nostalgic and reconnect with your younger self.

Give it your twist:
- Create an ultimate playlist.
- Visit an old favorite hang out place.
- Watch a themed movie marathon.

My experience:
Hour after hour my teenage self stayed in my room listening to rock albums. For a large block of those years, it was Led Zeppelin on the turntable. I would put on a stack of records at bedtime, and every twenty minutes or so a fresh side would drop down, so much variety and yet always so familiar.

The band influenced me in many ways. I read *The Hobbit* after dreaming of packing my bags for the Misty Mountains. I tracked down Willie Dixon and Muddy Waters records after listening to "You Shook Me" and "Whole Lotta Love." I grew to love Robert Johnson and Skip James. Not many shy, dorky suburban girls knew anything about the blues, so in addition to opening up a new world of music for me it also gave me a sort of niche when I really needed something to talk about and somewhere to belong.

My record collection had been in boxes with no way to play them for over a decade when we refinished our basement and got a turntable once again. I still listen to music a lot, but it's almost always in the background, in the car on the way to somewhere, or playing on my computer while I'm getting work done. It's rare that I will sit and really listen like I used to as a kid, when the only thing I did was look at the album cover or follow along with the lyrics, maybe doodling or writing in a journal too.

Most of my favorite artists came along into the digital era with me; I have CDs of Eric Clapton, the Band, Little Feat, Van Morrison, and the Beatles. For whatever reason, Zeppelin stayed in my past, so it brings up the most nostalgia when I hear them. For this reason, I decided to listen to all of my Led Zeppelin albums in a row.

I put on the first album. "In the days of my youth, I was told what it means to be a man...."

I am instantly brought back to my past, except there are no posters of Jim Morrison or unicorns on the walls, and my teenage boys are sitting beside me.

Enjoyment:	9/10
Difficulty:	1/10
Would I do it again?	Yes, the Beatles are in my sights.

14. Watch all of IMDb's Top 250 Movies

Why you should try it:
By watching everything on a list, you'll get exposed to movies that you probably never would have picked for yourself, and you just may love some of them.

Give it your twist:
- Watch the "50 Greatest Cult Movies of All Time."
- Read the top 20 of Modern Library's "100 Best Novels."
- Cook every entree in your favorite cookbook.

My experience:
In a world where Japanese movies reign supreme and World War II films fill the mailbox, one woman struggles on her couch to view them all.... That woman is this one... that quest is about to be challenged... and this time, it's personal....

I am a complete and utter movie fiend, so I was dismayed by how much I grew to dread the challenge of watching all of the IMDb Top 250 movies.

Frankly, I am glad the closing credits rolled on this project.

I shouldn't have been surprised that I loved so few of the 55 movies I hadn't yet seen from the list. I have spent over 30 years relishing movies, great and so-so alike, more if you count my childhood sitting by my father's side.

Whether spending an afternoon with Buster Keaton or a late night with Marlon Brando, my dad loved the classics, and I loved them right beside him. He would laugh himself silly over more modern movies, too. (I'll never be able to see Michael Caine sadistically whipping Steve Martin's legs in *Dirty Rotten*

Scoundrels without hearing my dad's laughter ringing in my head). He frequently had insomnia and would play an 8-hour tape of James Bond movies throughout the night, the theme song invading the dreams of my childhood as it bled through the bedroom walls.

I had hoped for some more hidden gems on the IMDb list, but it turned out that the chances were pretty good that if there was a movie I would love on the list, I had already seen it.

I enjoyed most of the movies enough to give them a viewing, but quite a few of them had me sleepy on the couch, struggling to stay awake. I did watch some while walking on the treadmill, just so you don't think I devolved into total couch-potatoness.

I give special awards to the following movies.

The "Hidden Gems" Award:
- *City of God*
- *Ikiru*
- *The Celebration*

The "Struggle to Stay Awake" Award:
- *Paths of Glory*
- *Das Boot*
- *Wild Strawberries*
- *Sunrise: A Song of Two Humans*
- *Ben-Hur*
- *Persona*
- *In the Mood for Love*
- *The Passion of Joan of Arc*

The "Couple of Great Scenes" Award:
- *Once Upon a Time in the West*
- *The Treasure of the Sierra Madre*
- *The Wages of Fear*
- *Night of the Hunter*

The "Give Me Two Hours of My Life Back" Award:
- *The Thing*

Really, how did *The Thing* show up on any list of greats?

Enjoyment: 5/10
Difficulty: 8/10
Would I do it again? No.

15. Make vegan cake pops

Why you should try it:
Trying to create something new under a set of restrictions can actually lead to more creativity.

Give it your twist:
- Make a "cream" sauce with no dairy.
- Create a meatless feast.
- Eat raw foods for a day.

My experience:
My entry in the vegan raw cake pop challenge:

Macadamia cherry chocolate vegan cake pops
- 1 1/2 cups raw macadamia nuts
- 1/3 cup unsweetened cocoa
- pinch salt
- 3/4 cup dried cherries
- 10 Medjool dates
- 1/2 teaspoon vanilla extract

I made a faux cream cheese frosting using Toffuti Better Than Cream Cheese, Earth Balance Spread, vanilla extract, and sweetener. I ground up the macadamia nuts with the salt and cocoa. I mixed in the cherries, dates, vanilla extract, and a little water, until it stuck together and could be formed into balls.

I formed the mixture into balls and froze them. I then applied the faux cream cheese frosting and froze them again. They were good. I liked the cake more than the frosting, though.

Note: After I entered the contest, I found out that the frosting was not raw because the ingredients were cooked during processing. A simple icing would work well for a raw topping.

Enjoyment: 7/10
Difficulty: 3/10
Would I do it again? Probably not, unless it was for a vegan guest.

16. Attend a New Year's celebration; kiss at midnight

Why you should try it:
It's fun to get out there on New Year's Eve (even though I also like being cozy at home and going to bed by 11).

Give it your twist:
- Go to Times Square on New Year's Eve.
- See the Macy's Thanksgiving Day Parade.
- Have paella at home at midnight.

My experience:
We brought in the new year with the Michael Cleary Band. Great show! We've been following Michael Cleary for 20 years, longer than that really because we followed him in his previous band, The Bus. We don't get out as much as we used to back in those days, but it was so much fun to ring in the new year at the show.

Enjoyment:	8/10
Difficulty:	2/10
Would I do it again?	I'd definitely see another show.

17. Try Zumba

Why you should try it:
Trying a new exercise class is a fun way to get a workout or shake-up your fitness routine, and dancing to music can make the minutes fly by.

Give it your twist:
- Try belly dancing.
- Take an aerial yoga class.
- Go Salsa dancing.

My experience:
I barely got a workout as I stood in my first Zumba class stepping a little in place, baffled by what to do. Every two seconds or so we switched to a new move. My strategy of hiding in the very back of the class worked for a while until we rotated 180 degrees, and I was then looking ridiculous in the front of the class. I was utterly unable to do the moves. At one point I was supposed to be skipping, and, paralyzed in place, all I could think was "C'mon! I know how to skip."

The instructor shouted out encouraging comments: "Here we go," "again," and "that's it," only it wasn't it. We hit flamenco, the Charleston, African dancing, and I don't even know what else.

I think she shouted "Bollywood" at one point, but I can't be sure.

I should have known I was in for this. I had tried the Kinect Dance Central game. I was quite hopeless at that, too, even when I set it to break down the moves and do them in slow motion.

My virtual instructor on the game would say to me, "Don't worry. It takes courage just to try."

Is it normal to get embarrassed by a cartoon character while alone in my basement?

Enjoyment: 1/10
Difficulty: 9/10
Would I do it again?   Never, ever!

18. Go snowboarding

Why you should try it:
It's fun to glide over the snow, and I hear that after a few tries most people can get the hang of it.

Give it your twist:
- Take a ski lesson.
- Try skateboarding.
- Make a hundred paper snowflakes.

My experience:
By the end of my first snowboarding lesson, I started to get a feel for turning, but my only way to stop was to fall. (I stopped a lot.)

During a 90-minute lesson, I only managed to stay upright for a few seconds at a time. It was fun to try. I found it a lot harder than skiing, but I have been told by many people that it usually takes a few tries to get the hang of it.

I was sore afterwards for days and days.

Enjoyment: 6/10
Difficulty: 9/10
Would I do it again? Maybe, but, oh, the aches and pains!

19. Ride a mechanical bull

Why you should try it:
Channel your inner cowboy (or whatever the current fad is) and try something new.

Give it your twist:
- Go horseback riding.
- Take a hip-hop dance class.
- Complete a tap dancing class.

My experience:
I have an inordinate love of the movie *Urban Cowboy*. Little did I realize that there is a full-fledged Gilley's-esque country Valhalla the next town over. When I found out they had a mechanical bull, I knew I had to try it.

Bud: "Ask me, 'How do you become a bull rider?'"

Friend: "How do you become a bull rider?"

Bud: "You take a handful of marbles, and you put 'em in your mouth. You go out to Gilley's, and you ride that bull, and every time you ride that bull you spit out one of those marbles, and when you've lost all your marbles, that's when you're a bull rider."

— *Urban Cowboy*

Getting on the bull was the hardest part. I was too short to get on easily, and then I jumped too much and slid off the other side a couple of times. I finally got the hang of it, though.

On my first ride, I made a classic rookie mistake, taking off my hat and trying to go one-handed. I hit the inflatable deck quickly. Second ride: a little better. Third ride: a little better again, but the guy still threw me very easily.

It was a blast. Afterwards, we played pool. We toyed with the idea of line dancing. Maybe next time.

Enjoyment: 8/10
Difficulty: 8/10
Would I do it again? Yes, so much fun.

See the video: http://www.tootimidandsqueamish.com/2011/05/ride-that-bull/

20. Give a sample from my gut (replacement task for giving blood)

Why you should try it:
Giving blood saves lives; giving a gut sample helps science.

Give it your twist:
- Give blood through NIH for research.
- Become an organ donor.
- Volunteer at a blood drive.

My experience:
My blood can't be completely trusted, at least for the foreseeable future, so I am going to give my gut.

American Gut is an open-source project where a wealth of data about the microbes in everyone's gut is shared with the world. Some of the information is bringing new attention to the idea that the American gut is in trouble. Decades of exposure to antibiotics (both prescribed and in the food chain) and eating of highly processed foods have reduced the biodiversity of the guts of average Americans as compared to the guts of people around the world who are eating a more traditional diet.

I made a donation and received a kit for giving my sample.

And my blood? It's probably fine, but I can't give to the American Red Cross for quite a while. I was banned from giving blood for one year after traveling to Costa Rica because of a small risk of carrying malaria; I was then banned for another year for traveling to Peru.

I will still give blood in the future once the CDC and I are sure that I am malaria-free.

Enjoyment: 5/10
Difficulty: 3/10
Would I do it again?   Maybe, it would be interesting after a dietary change.

21. Make eggplant lasagna

Why you should try it:
Making your own of something delicious is almost always easier than you might think.

Give it your twist:
- Make an easy lasagna toss.
- Try pumpkin lasagna.
- Bring lasagna rolls to a potluck.

My experience:
Eggplant lasagna was one of those things I always meant to try, but never got around to. It was easy and delicious.

Enjoyment: 5/10
Difficulty: 3/10
Would I do it again? Yes.

22. Complete a spontaneous challenge

Why you should try it:
If you do make a list of 101 things in 1001 days, save room for at least one spontaneous challenge. Once you're in the midst of your challenges, you may think of a new way to expand your comfort zone.

Give it your twist:
- What do you hold yourself back from doing? Things by yourself?
- Confront a fear.
- Sign up for an athletic competition that comes along.

My experience:
A murky understanding of a high school physics lesson is how I tend to think about my couch-potatoness: An object at rest tends to stay at rest. So I gave myself a challenge to get out and do three things on my own using Meetup.com. I enjoyed the social occasions: a book talk, a writer's group, and lunch at an Indian restaurant.

1. Book talk: *Half the Sky*
I joined a small group for a discussion of *Half the Sky*. This book disturbed and amazed me. The authors chronicle the stories of women around the world who have been victims of sex trafficking, bride burnings, war crimes, and medical neglect, but the book also offers uplifting stories of hope. I found the book inspiring and enjoyed the discussion. I will be joining the group again to discuss *Uncle Tom's Cabin*.

This was the easiest of the three events in that I am used to participating in book clubs, and the book itself gave the context for the discussion.

2. Writer's Group

While I am pretty comfortable with joining book group discussions, this one definitely took me out of my comfort zone. I met with a small group of writers, and we shared and discussed each other's writing. While I felt very shy, the group was supportive, and I plan on going back.

3. Restaurant lunch

This one was actually the hardest in that I felt nervous before I left, having to walk into a restaurant by myself to meet up with strangers. I needn't have worried. A few nice people were there, and we enjoyed chatting over a meal at an Indian restaurant.

While inertia tends to keep me at rest, now that I've gotten the ball rolling, I am hoping this trait of the law of motion also applies: an object in motion tends to stay in motion. A wine tasting and zorbing are in my future.

Enjoyment: 6/10
Difficulty: 9/10
Would I do it again? Yes, I have tried more Meetups.

23. Eat Pizza at Pepe's

Why you should try it:
What restaurant has the best of the best? Make up a reason to revisit a favorite place or discover a new one. Great food, great times.

Give it your twist:
- Ask around for places in your area that are supposedly the best.
- Have a showdown: Best burger, lobster roll, hot dog, or wings.
- Organize a cook-off at your home or workplace.

My experience:
On Wooster Street in New Haven are two famed New Haven pizza restaurants. New Haven-style pizza is cooked in a brick oven and noted for its thin crispy crust. Pepe's, the original from 1925, and Sally's, the newer kid on the block from 1938, regularly have long lines of patrons waiting for their pies. Locals argue about which one is better. I tried them on different nights with slightly different orders, so I know I am comparing eggplant to basil here, but this is how they stacked up.

Atmosphere: Sally's has an old-timey charm, with newspaper clippings on the wall and a dimly lit interior. It was easy to imagine Frank Sinatra biting into a slice. Pepe's has a similar decor, but is more upscale and more recently renovated. For the historical feel, I give the atmosphere edge to Sally's.

Service: At the time I went to Sally's in a party of four, there was no line (about 7 p.m. on a Wednesday night). We opened the door and walked in. Oops! We were supposed to wait outside and were gruffly told so by a waiter.

The waiter was well schooled in ignoring us when we wanted to put in new drink orders, too.

At Pepe's, on the other hand, we were greeted warmly. There was a large stop sign on the door indicating the "rules," so we knew to wait outside. We timed our visit to avoid lines (5 p.m. on a Thursday). I know the line waiting is part of the tradition, but it's just not our thing. Our waitress was extremely friendly and attentive. By the way, as we were exiting, we saw some new patrons walk right in through the stop sign, and they were asked to wait outside in a very friendly and helpful way. For service, Pepe's won by a mile.

Taste: It all really comes down to taste, right? Going in, I thought they both would be great, and they were, so it's hard to make the call.

At both places, we got a red pizza (eggplant parmesan at Sally's, Margherita at Pepe's) and a white clam pizza (with bacon at Sally's). They were all delicious — crispy chewy crusts, with fresh, flavorful toppings. For the red, I give the prize to Sally's. The red sauce was thicker and richer, and the creamy eggplant and mozzarella were perfect additions. Pepe's red was delicious, too, though; don't get me wrong.

The white: Pepe's white clam pizza was sublime. Huge, juicy chunks of freshly shucked clams were all over the pie, interspersed with big chunks of garlic and swimming in olive oil.

Sally's red won and Pepe's white won, a split decision. I award the taste prize to Pepe's, though, since its white was the overall winner. I usually don't even order white pizzas over red pizzas, but it won me over at the first bite.

The winner: Pepe's!

Enjoyment: 8/10
Difficulty: 1/10
Would I do it again? Yes, I have already.

24. Comment on 50 random blogs

Why you should try it:
There are great blogs out there for every possible interest, so explore a little.

Give it your twist:
- Start a blog.
- Follow a blog that focuses on a hobby of yours.
- Write the author of a blog who inspired you.

My experience:
I am often a lurker, but I have been working on commenting more often on the blogs that I come across in my browsing.

Enjoyment: 6/10
Difficulty: 7/10
Would I do it again? Sort of—I do leave comments more these days.

25. Influence a person to make a Day Zero list

Why you should try it:
Sharing your projects with the world can bring unexpected consequences.

Give it your twist:
- Make your own list of 101 things in 1001 days.
- Identify 40 things to do before you turn 40.
- Create a bucket list.

My experience:
At Day Zero, you can post your own list of 101 things in 1001 days and check out many ideas for bucket list items. I borrowed a lot of ideas that I found on the site, and I was excited when Shannon of *My Place in the Race* started her own list after reading about my quest.

Enjoyment: 7/10
Difficulty: 2/10
Would I do it again? No, I'm not planning on another list.

26. Make a soufflé

Why you should try it:
It's like magic when a soufflé comes out of the oven all puffed up.

Give it your twist:
- Make a sweet potato soufflé.
- Whip your own cream.
- Bake a custard.

My experience:
I had been baffled about what I did wrong during my chocolate soufflé attempt on Christmas day, but I very happily saw soft peaks form on my egg whites during my second soufflé attempt: Cheese soufflé.

Enjoyment:	7/10
Difficulty:	7/10
Would I do it again?	Yes, maybe chocolate will work next time?

27. Memorize a favorite poem

Why you should try it:
Give yourself a mental challenge. You'll feel sharper and more confident, or at least you'll be able to impress someone at a cocktail party.

Give it your twist:
- Complete crossword puzzles.
- Work your way through a Sudoku book.
- Learn 100 new vocabulary words.

My experience:
I chose "The Love Song of J. Alfred Prufrock" by T.S. Eliot to memorize because it takes me back to my first year of teaching.

A room of sweaty teenagers in dress shirts and ties, blouses and skirts, waited, pens poised, for me to write down what the poem meant on the blackboard so they could copy it neatly into their college-ruled notebooks. Not only did I not know what it meant, but what would be the point of telling them? It was their job to figure it out.

They became begrudgingly intrigued; during their years of education among nuns in a strict Catholic school, they had been trained not to speculate, not to come up with their own answers or even their own questions.

Back then, we had no Google ready to solve any mystery in 0.24 seconds; we were on our own. Their teenage minds could identify with being a specimen on a pin, with a "tedious argument of insidious intent," with mermaids who didn't sing to them.

Even if they didn't understand it, they got it.

"Do I dare disturb the universe?"

I also chose it since I have plenty of Prufrock in me, what with the whole "too timid" thing: "And indeed there will be time to wonder, 'Do I dare?' and 'Do I dare?' ... Do I dare to eat a peach?'"

Messing Up Prufrock

I failed at my first attempt to recite the poem on camera. Overly ambitious and under prepared, I had my husband walking backward through the yard while I followed, speaking into the camera. As if I wasn't struggling enough with all those pesky prepositions, I had to keep reacting to my husband's frantic gestures that I slow down as I strode toward him. It made me feel nervous and silly, and once I started laughing, I couldn't stop. After making it through most of the poem, I had just a few short stanzas left, and I felt the pressure mounting.

I messed up on a grand scale, making the bloopers video much more enjoyable than the real thing.

Enjoyment: 3/10
Difficulty: 8/10
Would I do it again?   Sure, but not with such a long poem.

See the videos: http://www.tootimidandsqueamish.com/2012/06/begrudgingly-intrigued-teenagers-j-alfred-prufrock/

28. Visit a UNESCO World Heritage Site

Why you should try it:
Chances are there is a World Heritage Site near you, and you can also check the list before you travel to find places with cultural or natural importance.

Give it your twist:
- Search for "things to do" in your area to find someplace new.
- Plan a trip around a site you've always dreamed of seeing.
- Follow a historic route.

My experience:
In the presence of the Parthenon, disappointment stabbed me.

Finally in Athens, I climbed the hill to the Acropolis in the extreme heat of the afternoon. I passed through the ornate gate, and, lifting my eyes toward this majestic temple to Athena, a giant crane greeted me. Camera poised, I circled what was left of the Parthenon, trying to find an angle that matched my mind's eye's view.

Sometimes the postcards are better than the real thing.

So after my family and I spent a hot Athenian morning that stretched into a hot Athenian afternoon, we made it back to our hotel exhausted, and I hatched a new plan. The next day we would sleep in, relax at our hotel's rooftop pool, walk the mile to the city in the late afternoon, and get to experience Athens at night.

We would climb Filopappos Hill, and we would look across a valley to see the Parthenon lit up against the pitch-black sky. My imagination was alive again. The universe owed me an awe-inspiring Parthenon moment, and I was going to get it.

We started up the hill in the late afternoon, an easy climb up a rocky path, everything going according to plan.

Then the problems started. My husband noticed that the path wasn't lighted. If we waited for the dark, we would be stumbling along the rocks on the way down. We, of course, had no flashlights, as we never do when flashlights are needed.

Now I may be timid and squeamish and all, but once I latch onto a plan, I will follow it to the Gates of Hades, a character trait that I both admire and hate about myself.

I can be obstinate. I can make bad decisions. I can insist we stay on the hill and wait for the sun to set, no matter how worried my husband is about the failing light or how bored my kids are that the sun has not gone down as quickly as I promised.

Eventually, the sun began to set, as it must, and streaks of gold and orange filled the sky. We sat and waited and posed for pictures, but confronted by this beauty, three of the four of us were grumpy, bored, impatient.

I wheedled and pleaded and got my husband and kids to wait an extra half-hour.

"Let's go," one of them whined, yet again.

The sun took its time, inching its way like a garbage truck blocking my lane during a busy commute.

"Just ten more minutes," I bargained.

My ten minutes long gone, lights finally appeared across the valley in the dusk. It wasn't dark yet, but it would have to do. When the lights flicker on at the Parthenon, pretty good is good enough, and keeping the peace is all the perfection you need.

I snapped my picture and agreed to hit the trail, tripping over rocks occasionally on my way down in the dimness. Nobody twisted an ankle that he would hold against me, and we walked the mile back to our hotel in peaceful quiet.

I took the elevator up to the roof alone. And I saw the Parthenon, there, off in the distance, glowing in the blackness, majestic.

Enjoyment:	8/10
Difficulty:	3/10
Would I do it again?	Yes, so many places to see.

29. Bake bread from scratch again

Why you should try it:
Nothing is quite like the aroma of baking bread. And, oh, to have some warm from the oven.

Give it your twist:
- Try a "quick bread" and you won't need to deal with yeast.
- Use whole wheat flour.
- Make homemade biscuits.

My experience:
What's better than making homemade butter? Having it on homemade bread, of course!

I used a basic white bread recipe from good old Betty Crocker. First, I mixed up the ingredients: flour, sugar, salt, shortening, yeast, and water.

(I so love that that's it for the ingredients! I had been reading labels a lot, trying to cut down on processed foods. For this bread, I went with white flour, but I would like to start making whole wheat bread.)

Next step: kneading. The dough ball transforms from a sticky, lumpy mess to a wonderful, elastic plaything.

It doubled in size in about an hour. My favorite part: punching down the dough. (I needed to get out my frustration from a push-ups fail earlier in the day.)

I formed two loaves and let them rise again.
Then, they were ready for baking. Oh, the aroma!
We had some still warm, fresh from the oven.
We had some more with our Sunday dinner: crock pot chicken, brown rice, and broccoli.
What to do with the leftover bread? French toast!

Enjoyment: 6/10
Difficulty: 5/10
Would I do it again? Yes, I'd like to get a bread machine.

30. Travel alone at least overnight

Why you should try it:
Traveling with my family is one of my greatest joys, but I should be able to get a cab on my own, right? Traveling alone scared me immensely, but it also empowered me.

Give it your twist:
- Go to a party alone.
- Sign up for a Meetup in your area.
- Eat dinner at a nice restaurant alone.

My experience:
"Do one thing every day that scares you." — Eleanor Roosevelt

I don't know whether I can say I am too timid and squeamish any longer.

I can say that I followed Eleanor Roosevelt's advice during my solo trip to Costa Rica, except that on some of the days I did two or three things that scared me!

Here are a few of the things that took me way out of my comfort zone:
- Whitewater river rafting on the Rio Balsa (Class IV rapids)
- Rappelling down waterfalls
- Zip lining, including a kilometer-long Superman line
- Salsa dancing in front of a group, with the directions all in Spanish
- The whole experience of traveling alone

Pura Vida

These adventures were scary and crazy fun, but they also helped me to realize something. I am a different person than I was when I started my list, when I found it so difficult to go somewhere on my own or try something new.

During the trip, I learned to say "Pura Vida," a Costa Rican expression that means "this is living" or "awesome." I heard it throughout Costa Rica, a beautiful country of friendly, laid-back people, and it perfectly sums up my feelings about the amazing experience of taking a trip by myself.

Enjoyment: 10/10
Difficulty: 9/10
Would I do it again?   Yes, but my husband should get a turn.

31. Record a song with me playing a bodhrán with my family

Why you should try it:
Think of something new you saw on a vacation, and figure out how to try it at home; it'll give you a deeper connection to that special trip.

Give it your twist:
- Make gelato.
- Go out for espresso.
- Create your own sushi.

My experience:
Squeezed into a little Irish pub, a pub that looked exactly like what a movie set of an Irish pub would look like, I held my pint and smiled. This was the Ireland of my dreams and one of the moments I had come across an ocean for. The session unfolded before us, classic Irish music, but modern too. Young people with old souls played and played, musicians sitting in and leaving frequently in fluid groupings.

The moment at this music festival coalesced into perfection: joyful music, an adoring crowd, my children and husband with me on our first international trip.

In a pause between songs, an Irish gentleman sitting at the bar broke out into a ballad, filling the room with his baritone, filling my heart with a happiness that seemed to reach back for generations into my family's past.

The session musicians started again. The young man on the bodhrán, an Irish drum, struck me the most as he played with exuberant abandon.

So a bodhrán was carried by me from Ireland to the U.S. and put upon my wall. I vowed to play it one day.

One of my sons plays the clarinet, one the violin, and my husband plays guitar, so I took the drum in our little quartet. We hammered out a version of "Molly Malone," the tart with the cart. I cannot hold a rhythm to the amazement of my naturally talented family. They played along the best they could.

It wasn't pretty, but it was sweet.

Enjoyment:	6/10
Difficulty:	9/10
Would I do it again?	Lord, no.

32. Walk 10,000 steps a day for an average of six days a week

Why you should try it:
Setting a goal to do something nearly every day will help you to establish a habit. If you get a good streak going, you won't want to break it, giving you a lot of motivation.

Give it your twist:
- Drink a certain amount of water each day.
- Exercise at least three days a week.
- Floss every night.

My experience:
I love a good streak.

I walked at least 10,000 steps a day for over a thousand days in a row. Now, I know that's the minimum recommendation for movement in a day, but it took a lot of effort to be that consistent.

I felt myself going through four distinct phases in adopting this habit.

Enthusiastic Beginner
I started walking around my neighborhood when the weather was nice. There was enough daylight after dinner to take a pleasant stroll. I listened to new music podcasts, and the miles just flew by. It was only when it was raining hard that I had to get creative and do things like walk at the mall before dinner, after ordering, and after dinner to get the steps in.

Struggling Beginner

The days grew short and cold. It was hard to always get the steps in. I don't have sidewalks in my area, and I tried walking the narrow, snow-filled roads only a few times before I decided that was too dangerous. We were having our basement done with plans to get a treadmill, and I just had to hang in there. There were delays and delays and delays. These were the dark days of keeping my streak alive.

Intermediate Habit Former

Once I hit 100 days in a row, I told myself I wouldn't obsess about whether I got 10,000 steps or not on a particular day because it's an arbitrary goal that doesn't really matter. Yeah, that didn't really happen. I wanted the steps, and I did anything to get them. I took laps around my living room/kitchen/dining room circuit while my family was watching TV, which meant that about every eight seconds I walked in front of them. Sorry! On the day of a road trip down to D.C. after work, I walked the streets in clogs during my lunch break and then had to walk a Virginian parking lot during a dinner break on the road. On a bitterly cold and windy night, we rushed down to New Haven to meet people when I still needed another mile or so, and I ventured out of the restaurant on my own for a chilly jaunt.

Habitual Walker

Once the treadmill was up and running and the habit was in place, walking just became a regular part of my day. Some days I get up a little early, some days I walk before dinner, and some days I finish up before bed. It just feels right to get at least that much activity in every day, and I love a good walk to clear my head after a stressful day.

I keep a pedometer in my pocket, and the common advice that's shared all the time really is true. Tips like taking the stairs, parking farther away from the store, and getting up from the computer periodically all add up. I have a pretty sedentary job, so I usually only have about two miles in at the end of a school day. That leaves about three miles to get in on the treadmill or during a walk after school.

I tend to be an all-or-nothing kind of a person, so I worried that if I ended the streak, I would instantly become a couch potato again. Now, though, I think the habit is well ingrained. One day my streak will inevitably have to end, and the next day will be day number one.

Enjoyment:	7/10
Difficulty:	8/10
Would I do it again?	Yes, it's a habit now.

33. Paint the garage doors

Why you should try it:
Tackling a neglected chore can give you a lot of satisfaction. Painting my garage doors was one of those for me, but my plans took a strange turn.

Give it your twist:
- Clean out your closets.
- Renovate a bathroom.
- Get new kitchen cabinets.

My experience:
I complained to my husband about our peeling, rotting garage doors.
His reply: "So fix them."

I gave him a confused look and explained: "It's my job to point out things that need to be fixed and your job to fix them."

He wasn't buying it, which was how #33 on my list of 101 things became "Paint the garage doors." I would be able to procrastinate for quite a long time, but not forever.

Soon there was a problem. First one door, then the other, broke. We would need new garage doors, so it really made no sense to fix and paint the old ones. I had to, though, because it was on my list. What to do?

Graffiti to the Rescue!
I needed to spray paint graffiti on them, of course.

What fast-motion video would be complete without the theme from the "Benny Hill Show" to accompany it?

See the video: http://www.tootimidandsqueamish.com/2012/11/graffiti-to-the-rescue-i-tag-my-garage/

I restored the doors to respectability pretty quickly. The irony was not lost on me that I was too timid to leave them proudly on display for the neighborhood. I was concerned, though, that some kind soul would worry that I really had been vandalized and call the police, or that someone would be outraged while trying to sell a house on the street. (It would still be a while before our new doors were installed.)

I hastily slapped on some old white paint, just enough to keep away the police.

Enjoyment: 8/10
Difficulty: 7/10
Would I do it again? No, the new doors are finally installed.

34. Take an art class

Why you should try it:
Trying something that you know you have no talent for can help you to understand the risks others take, and, who knows? You just might like it.

Give it your twist:
- Learn to read 50 Chinese characters.
- Try Bikram yoga.
- Take a snowboarding lesson.

My experience:
Pushing past the black cloth that blocked the room from the street, my friend and I clutched our sketchpads and entered the den of artists. The nude model was on a break and all the chairs were filled, so a kind man found us a low table and placed it right up front, inviting us to sit on the floor in front of all the real artists.

Uh, no.

We found a spot on the bay window in back and stayed as unobtrusive as possible.

The model disrobed, and we got to work. In her first pose, she tucked her legs underneath her and leaned back on her arms. I struggled to try to capture her form; her face and hands were beyond me.

The atmosphere in the room was hushed and serious as the artists worked on their sketches. The organizer played various recordings of poetry readings. I caught snippets of "muscatel" and "Larimer" and felt I was *On the Road* again with Kerouac.

My friend and I worked quietly throughout the 20-minute pose. When it was time to show each other our work, I wished I could reveal something like Picasso's *Lying Female Nude with Cat*.

But there was no cat.

During the second pose, the model sat cross-legged with her hands in her lap. The mood took a surreal turn as I recognized the words in the next poem: "Mars ain't the kind of place to raise your kids. In fact it's cold as hell." It was William Shatner reciting Elton John's "Rocket Man."

The second pose was 20 minutes also, but the time passed much more quickly as I was more focused and pulled into the task.

Aside from some initial awkwardness and feelings of intimidation, I liked this experience of getting out of my comfort zone to try to draw, something I have rarely done since my last junior high school art class.

And that class certainly didn't feature any nude models.

Enjoyment:	6/10
Difficulty:	7/10
Would I do it again?	Probably not.

35. Volunteer at a soup kitchen or homeless shelter

Why you should try it:
There are people in need all over. Give a hand.

Give it your twist:
- Organize a food drive.
- Go on a mitten run.
- Round up your unused clothing to donate.

My experience:
I chopped potatoes and carrots for a gigantic pot of soup to be served to those in need in New Haven, CT. I joined a friendly group of volunteers who got the meal ready efficiently.

Enjoyment: 6/10
Difficulty: 3/10
Would I do it again? Yes.

36. Watch the sunrise and sunset in the same day

Why you should try it:
Start and end your day connected to nature.

Give it your twist:
- Go on an overnight hike.
- Paint a sunrise.
- Collect 20 different types of leaves.

My experience:
"Life is a journey, not a destination."
— Ralph Waldo Emerson

The final section of hiking the Inca Trail in Peru was a surreal experience, part race, part circus.

We had gotten up at 3 a.m. to try to be the first group in the queue to register at the checkpoint, which opened at 5:30 a.m.

Upon awakening, I choked down a little bread and jam and a few sips of a thin quinoa porridge. I had not had an appetite for days, whether from the high altitude or the pills I was taking to prevent altitude sickness, or both, I don't know, but I had an aversion to eating and felt depleted and weak.

I was also, though, at the point of being the most acclimated to the altitude and had four days of rigorous hiking behind me, so I was also feeling at my strongest.

We had prepared everything the night before, so the next thing I knew after making some instant coffee that was too blazingly hot to drink, I was rushing through the darkness, still half asleep and feeling miserable.

We arrived at the checkpoint at 3:32 a.m. — the first group of the 15 or so groups at the campsite — and we briefly celebrated before settling down for two hours on a cold bench to wait for the checkpoint to open. The next group came in eight minutes after us, so there hadn't been much time to spare.

We were first in the queue to hike to the Sun Gate. If we hiked slowly, the hikers behind us could pass us, so we were motivated to hike our fastest. (Lining up behind many groups as they took photos at the Sun Gate would delay our entry to Machu Picchu until after the sunrise and the hordes of tourists arriving by train and bus. Hikers: don't you hate it when a busload of people are crowding the destination you've worked so hard to hike to?)

I sat cold on the bench in a nauseated, foggy daze until about 5:10 a.m., when my group started to prepare for the final section of our Inca Trail hike. One member of the group played music on his phone, and another led us in some gentle stretches. There were groans all around at our various aches and pains from three days on the trail.

My son David encouraged me, knowing my slower than average pace: "Mom, just go ham. You can take a break when you're done. Just push yourself, OK?"

Our guide spurred us on as well: "This is the moment you've been training for. Find your rhythm and try to keep it up without stopping."

A pre-race atmosphere clearly established, it took only a few minutes for our documents to be checked at 5:30. A starting gun may as well have sounded because I shot off into the darkness, suddenly invigorated and keeping up with the fast hikers in our group.

Most of this section of the trail was a smooth dirt path, heaven compared to the stone steps and jagged rocks we had spent so much time on. While the long-legged people strode ahead, I jogged on my short legs through the darkness with only my headlamp pointing out the obstacles as they rushed up to meet me. I was breathing heavily but rhythmically and enjoying the thrill of going as fast as I could with a graceful ease I had not yet felt on the trail. I kept this pace for perhaps 40 minutes when I slowed down on the steep, final climb to the Sun Gate.

At the Sun Gate, our whole group celebrated with high fives and congratulations for hiking the Inca Trail. We posed for pictures with Machu Picchu in the mist behind us before hurrying on to walk the final mile or so down to the site.

On our way, we saw the sun rise over a mountain, and the ancient city of Machu Picchu slowly lit up.

Conclusion

Hiking the Inca Trail was, for me, a difficult physical challenge, as I knew it would be, but it was an emotional challenge as well. I dealt with sleeping in a tent, not always having the right gear, preparing for bed after dinner in the dark, changes in temperature from cold to hot to cold again, tossing and turning through the night knowing I would need every bit of energy I could summon each morning, losing my appetite and feeling exhausted, getting a persistent cough, gasping in the high altitude, worrying about my kids (although they were much stronger than I).... All of these things added to the challenge, but they added to the sense of accomplishment as well.

We hiked as part of a great group of people. Our guides, porters, and chefs worked hard to make our hike a success.

Finally at the "lost city" of the Incas, I enjoyed the guided tour, but what will most stand out in my memory is the first glimpse of the ancient city in the mist as I rushed through the Sun Gate, the hardest physical challenge of my life accomplished, and my family and new friends there to celebrate it with me.

Later in the day, as the group sat exhausted in a minibus returning to Cuzco, we saw the sun set over the mountains, just about twelve hours after we had seen it rise over Machu Picchu. It was time to rest.

Enjoyment:	9/10
Difficulty:	9/10
Would I do it again?	Yes (as long as it wasn't that difficult)!

Read about the rest of my days on the Inca Trail:
http://www.tootimidandsqueamish.com/2013/08/hiking-the-inca-trail-day-1-peruvian-flatlands/

37. Try to grow tomatoes again

Why you should try it:
Growing your own food can be healthy, economic, and satisfying.

Give it your twist:
- Plant an herb garden.
- Try an upside down tomato planter.
- Start a compost bin.

My experience:
I had failed at growing tomatoes in containers the previous summer. After buying containers and potting soil, I only managed to grow one $50 tomato. I was determined to try it again. This time, I had some modest success; the best part, though, was goofing around with my son for a photo by having him eat one fresh off the vine. Now that's a fresh tomato!

Enjoyment:	6/10
Difficulty:	7/10
Would I do it again?	Probably not.

38. Don't complain about anything for a week

Why you should try it:
So many of our days are consumed by negativity, and a lot of the complaints accomplish nothing and are just a bad habit. Do you have any bad habits you can try to confront?

Give it your twist:
- Pick a bad habit to focus on for a week.
- Give up social media for a week.
- Avoid sarcastic comments for a week.

My experience:
I survived a frustrating computer lab fiasco without complaining, only to be done in by ice cream, so I started over. And over. And over.

On my first day, I felt pretty good getting through an entire school day without complaining, but I quickly discovered there are a lot of gray areas. What exactly constitutes a complaint? While some complaints are instantly recognizable, in other situations I may be rightly asserting myself. Is it the tone that makes it a complaint? The repetition?

Then I posted a cartoon on Facebook, and a colleague who knew about my challenge ruled it a complaint. I countered that I was expressing myself through art, as artists have done through the ages. I suppose Picasso was complaining when he created *Guernica*, eh? She didn't buy it.

That debate became moot the same night when I muttered to my husband, "Why didn't you get something with chocolate in it?" when he surprised us with ice cream, and I was busted on Day 2.

I started over and got tripped up again on my new Day 2 when there was some miscommunication about a track practice pickup. Then when my husband came home late on a night we had dinner plans, I had to start yet again.

I finally made it through this challenge, or did I? I might have just relaxed the rules on what counts as a complaint. I did make some improvements in avoiding "venting" at work. Let's face it: venting doesn't do anybody any good.

Four typical learning phases:
1. Unconscious incompetence
2. Conscious incompetence
3. Conscious competence
4. Unconscious competence

I think at best I was entering Phase 2: conscious incompetence. I made a little progress and felt myself letting go of grievances more easily. I will try to keep the better habit going now that I am free to complain again.

I might have to stay away from the computer lab, though.

Enjoyment:	5/10
Difficulty:	7/10
Would I do it again?	Yes, it's a work in progress.

39. Go to Greece

Why you should try it:
Take a vacation you've always dreamed of.
Give it your twist:
- Visit all 50 U.S. states.
- Go to a Greek festival.
- Cook a Greek feast.

My experience:
During our vacation in Greece, we spent a few days in Athens on our own before sailing through the islands on a yacht as part of a small group, and we finished up on our own for a few days in Santorini.

It was a wonderful trip. Greece is a beautiful country with an inspiring history, a relaxed pace, and great food. Some of my favorite moments were walking through the steep, winding streets of small villages and glimpsing the little moments of village life — people hanging out their laundry, chatting on their steps, laughing in *tavernas*, gathering up their kids, or herding their goats.

Enjoyment:	9/10
Difficulty:	4/10
Would I do it again?	Yes, but there are many new places to go.

40. Send a secret to PostSecret

Why you should try it:
Writing down a secret and sending it off can be liberating.

Give it your twist:
- Do three acts of kindness secretly.
- Send a love letter in a secret code.
- Call someone up to apologize for an old wrong.

My experience:
My lips are sealed on this one, but I popped my secret into a mailbox at the post office, and I felt the tiniest lightening of a burden.

Inspired by PostSecret, a site that publishes people's anonymous handmade postcards of their secrets, I invite people to send me handmade postcards that celebrate times they've gone outside of their comfort zones.

How about you: Send me a postcard? More information: http://www.tootimidandsqueamish.com/send-me-your-postcard/

Enjoyment: 3/10
Difficulty: 5/10
Would I do it again? No.

41. Read Anna Karenina

"Happy families are all alike; every unhappy family is unhappy in its own way."
-- Leo Tolstoy

Why you should try it:
Is there a classic you were supposed to read in high school but didn't? Give it another try; you might love it.

Give it your twist:
- See Russian dancers.
- Read *War and Peace*.
- Watch *Doctor Zhivago*.

My experience:
Trying to call up an old memory is like checking my wrist for the time and realizing I haven't worn a watch in years. I stare blankly, trying to remember what I was looking for, but it's not there anymore.

Lately, though, I have been awash in words to describe the snippets and fragments of my past.

It started in my car.

I commute at least an hour each workday, a grind that makes me regret the lost time; I've been doing it for 20 years, though, so any day now I should start getting used to it.

At least I figured out a way to finally finish *Anna Karenina*, which I had started two years earlier for a book club meeting but had to return to the library way before I finished its 800 pages. By getting it on discs (count 'em, 30!), my terrible commute became a pleasure with time at last to read.

I always read at bedtime, but on most nights I get about six minutes in before my head starts to nod. It's a blessing to be able to fall asleep so easily, but it sure doesn't help the carriage wheels turn through the cobblestoned streets of Moscow and Saint Petersburg.

The miles roll by while I am listening in the car, and I have more ideas for writing than ever before. Seeing these sentences lingering by the dashboard somehow triggers half-forgotten memories, and they rise up in vivid sentences. It happened with an Ernest Hemingway book, too. The odd thing is that my ideas are completely unrelated to the book being played. I have just as few memories in 19th century Russian drawing rooms as I have hunting on the *Green Hill of Africa*, but my mind starts writing vignettes from my past.

As the CD spins, I'll get lost in a daydream and unconsciously compose a few paragraphs about my own life. I'll rewind the disc to find out what's happened, but these called-up memories are captured like perfectly pinned butterflies until I have a chance to jot them down.

In my commuting switch to literature, I abandoned the news on NPR, at least for now. I am not as up on the sequester as I would have been, but I have bits of memoir scribbled on my scrap paper and Russian patronymics rolling off my tongue.

Enjoyment:	8/10
Difficulty:	6/10
Would I do it again?	No.

42. Have a Philly cheesesteak

Why you should try it:
In between your other activities, investigate a city's most famous delicacy and decide for yourself which one is the best.

Give it your twist:
- Have deep-dish pizza in Chicago.
- Go to Boston for baked beans.
- Get a po-boy sandwich in New Orleans.

My experience:
Strolling through a park on a pleasant summer's afternoon in Philly, I heard out of the corner of my ear a pronounced, "Ah, now Boston is not entirely fashionable." I turned, and a woman dressed in a gown and petticoat with a tricorn hat was looking our way. Someone was dissing my Dan, 18th century style.

Dan had been getting it all day. He was wearing a Red Sox tee shirt on day three of a three-day series against the Phillies, and locals were gleefully (and gently) teasing him about the two games the Sox had already lost.

We walked to Reading Terminal Market, where we had our first Philly cheesesteak at Carmen's. I got mine with provolone and mushrooms, onions, and peppers.

The Red Sox won the game 5-2. Locals were a little quieter after that.

After the game, we headed to the legendary Pat's to try the original cheesesteak. I liked Carmen's sandwich better, but everyone else liked Pat's.

From our hotel, we walked about a mile to the Philadelphia Museum of Art, where Rocky ran up the steps. It was a fun place to goof around, with a lot of visitors running up. Dan left me in his dust as he lightly jogged up the steps with me trailing behind. It still felt triumphant to get up to the top and raise my arms in victory.

On day two, we slept in and then walked to the Franklin Institute, where we saw the Mummies exhibit and the rest of the museum.

Before heading back, we managed to eat one more sandwich, roast pork at DiNic's. Some say the roast pork sandwich is vying with the cheesesteak for the spot of Philly's signature sandwich. Roasted pork with provolone and garlicky broccoli rabe — it was my favorite of the three sandwiches we tried.

It was a great visit. I loved the city, very friendly and much less crowded than New York. And I hear there's a cannoli I have got to try.

Enjoyment: 8/10
Difficulty: 1/10
Would I do it again?   Oh, yeah.

43. Try at least five new recipes while eating vegetarian for a week

Why you should try it:
Setting a goal to try new recipes can break you out of a rut of always cooking the same old things. If you don't do it already, try adding a vegetarian night or two to your week.

Give it your twist:
- Go vegan for a week.
- Try a new recipe from Pinterest one night a week.
- Add a new vegetable dish to your repertoire each week.

My experience:
I ate vegan for a week, and I felt great and learned a lot, but I had more than a couple boring meals. Since then, I try to eat vegetarian at least once a week, and I eat less meat when I eat other meals.

Hoping to expand my options, I built a week of vegetarian eating around trying some new recipes.

1. Baked Falafel with Tzatziki
I love falafel and had never tried making it at home. This baked version was great, and the tzatziki was easy and delicious, too. I served them with pitas and a lot of toppings for dinner, and I had them over spinach in a salad for lunch the next day.

2. Spinach Cashew Cream Pasta

This vegan recipe used cashews instead of dairy for its delicious, nutritious creaminess. I make pasta sauce a lot, but I always make it very chunky on the stove top, cooking it for hours. I loved this technique of food processing the ingredients before cooking for a quick alternative.

3. Channa Masala

This spicy Indian chickpea dish was delicious, and I loved the easy-to-follow directions. I topped it with yogurt and served it with brown rice, broccoli, naan, and mango.

4. Sweet Potato and Caramelized Onion Quesadillas

The combination of sweet potatoes, caramelized onions, and cheese in these quesadillas was very flavorful. I served them with chunky guacamole and brown rice. Nobody missed the meat.

5. The Green Monster

I had been wanting to try a Green Monster for a while. I combined spinach with almond milk, lemon yogurt, banana, mango, and a little peanut butter. There is a whole "Green Monster Movement" where people post their variation of this smoothie. I kept thinking of an old joke from *Cheers* — "You can really taste the kale!" — even though it was spinach and wasn't very noticeable. I thought it made a refreshing snack. My son was not very enthusiastic, but he did manage to smile in one photo.

I loved the variety of these easy and delicious recipes and will be adding them to my family menus.

Enjoyment: 6/10
Difficulty: 5/10
Would I do it again? Yes, I'm always looking for new recipes.

44. Relearn "Greensleeves" on guitar

Why you should try it:
Revisit one of your teenage aspirations.

Give it your twist:
- Learn a song on the harmonica.
- Take a jazz dance class.
- Paint a portrait of someone you love.

My experience:
"Alas, my love, you do me wrong,
To cast me off discourteously."
– Greensleeves

Back in high school, it was a struggle of love to show up for guitar lessons each week, paid for myself out of a scant minimum wage. I had no rhythm to speak of and was unable to find a correct note, but I loved music so much that I dreamed that I could one day play.

After picking my way haltingly through "Mary Had a Little Lamb," my lack of ability was clear, but I stuck with it lesson after lesson, hardly ever able to turn the page to a new ditty. When I finally arrived at the hauntingly beautiful "Greensleeves," though, I found a new enthusiasm.

I barricaded myself in my room and played only that one song over and over, slowly working out my first chords. I practiced until I could play it by heart and just about keep the time too — well, all except for a pesky F sharp on the fourth fret that my little pinky could never quite reach. I showed up for my next guitar lesson and performed the whole song from memory for my teacher.

I eventually decided classical guitar wasn't for me and begged him to teach me how to "just play," visions of leading sing-alongs of "Do Wah Diddy" around a campfire were plucked out in my head. That never happened. I cannot sing either and never got the hang of playing. My guitar collected dust for thirty years, but "Greensleeves" remained for me a pure moment of musical joy.

A month ago I pulled my guitar out, dusted it off, and tried to learn to play again. I suffered through the basics, back with Mary and her lamb. Mired in frustration, I flipped forward 40 pages to take a peek at the prize, "Greensleeves."

I didn't remember how to read most of the music, so after painstakingly looking up each note in each chord, I began to play it again. To my surprise, my fingers ignored my scribbled notes and magically went to the right spots on their own, muscle memory awakened after a 30-year slumber. Well, except for that F sharp that my husband heard me miss so many times that he asked if it was the F.U. sharp.

After running through it over and over, I had it down, not perfect by any means, but a song I could play by heart. Just don't expect "Do Wah Diddy" around the campfire anytime soon.

Enjoyment:	8/10
Difficulty:	7/10
Would I do it again?	Yes.

See the video: http://www.tootimidandsqueamish.com/2013/10/greensleeves/

45. Have dinner by candlelight

Why you should try it:
Breaking out the candles can give that dinner the romantic mood you're hoping for (or it can really help when the power is out).

Give it your twist:
- Make your own candles.
- Have a gourmet meal in complete darkness.
- Create a centerpiece using pinecones and walnuts.

My experience:
See #99: Give up caffeine for a day.

Enjoyment: 5/10
Difficulty: 6/10
Would I do it again? Yes, but hopefully by choice.

46. Declutter my house

Why you should try it:
Your closets and drawers are probably filled with things that just get in your way, and other people may be able to make use of them.

Give it your twist:
- Organize a closet.
- Makeover a spare room.
- Keep your counters clutter-free for one month.

My experience:
See that little piece of wood with nails pounded into it? I don't know what it is or why I saved it, so as I worked through the last cluttered area of my house, it was safe to say it was time to toss it.

My closets and drawers were overstuffed with such items, and although I've been a pack rat for years, I've been learning to let go.

Several of the tasks on my list of 101 things in 1001 days were about getting rid of things:
- 46: Declutter my house.
- 55: Play, give away, or throw out each of the 32 board games in my basement.
- 72: Go through the basement bins and donate, sell, or throw out what I can.
- 88: Give away or throw out the collection of stained glass pieces in the basement.
- 98: Sell some more Elks pins on eBay.

As I worked to declutter the drawer beside my bed, I was struck by how useless most of the things were: a direct deposit notice from a paycheck in 2005, a photocopied list of addresses and phone numbers on which the only name I could recognize was my own, little containers of buttons, and so forth.

I decluttered various closets and drawers over the last year or so. I gave away a lot of stuff through Freecycle and Goodwill. I also made about $1,000 selling some of my old stuff on eBay; aside from the money, I like the idea of people getting use out of the things rather than having them collecting dust and taking up space.

I've also been working to simplify my life. I am tempted along with everyone else to get the latest gadget, but by avoiding new purchases and streamlining my lifestyle, I've set aside most of my disposable income for travel. I would rather spend money on a new experience than a new thing, and my husband and I have eliminated gift-giving as much as possible in favor of doing things together.

And that mysterious wood and nail object pictured above? Once I snapped a picture of it to be emblematic of the useless things I've saved, I found I had formed an attachment to it. I tucked it back into my now spacious bedside drawer.

Enjoyment:	2/10
Difficulty:	8/10
Would I do it again?	Yes, I'm sure I'll need to.

47. Jump off a cliff

Why you should try it:
Confront a fear. Hear yourself roar.
Give it your twist:
- Bungee jump.
- Skydive.
- Give a speech.
My experience:
"Some people think it's holding that makes one strong. Sometimes it's letting go."
— Unknown

I hold onto things fiercely: movie ticket stubs, anger, prints of bad photos, grudges, logs of old exercise routines, worries, and, especially, the ground beneath my feet.

I've been getting better at letting go, but I still catch myself hoarding, whether it's useless things or useless feelings.

For example, the moment my cutting board pushed the handmade garlic holder off the counter and I saw it shatter into pieces, I burst into tears. I remembered my dad, who has since passed away, writing the word "garlic" into the soft clay. I tucked the broken pieces into a drawer and couldn't throw them out — for years. I finally hit upon a compromise. I took a photo of the word my dad had drawn and threw out the pieces.

I'm learning that it's sometimes better to just let go.

At a recreation park, my kids waited in the water for me to jump off a cliff. I had climbed up feeling confident, but then I retreated from the edge. I needed a minute. And another. And five more. Why had I put this on my list? It would be so easy to back away, to go down the slide, to swim in the cool water.

I did it though. A moment of terror, an exhilarating plunge. It was intensely exciting, but I was glad it was over.

Jumping off a cliff

Our basement storage area had gotten so crammed that we could not maneuver through it any longer. I finally cleared out about ten bins of old stuff. Most of it had been untouched since I had carted it from the storage area of my previous house. It was time to just let go.

I saved some favorite books and toys from when my kids were small. I made up boxes of anything that could be donated. Most of it, though, was just junk.

A suede jacket that had walked the neighborhoods of my adolescence, along with a tattered jean jacket and a faded peach prom dress, all joined a broken-down rocking horse and piles of un-stuffed stuffed animals in the dumpster.

When they hooked up the dumpster to pull it away, part of me wondered why I had ever saved these things; most of me felt of wave of sadness to say goodbye. I also felt a lightness of spirit, though. Sometimes you have to just let go.

I still have a ways to go. Somewhere in my house is a little container of old baby teeth.

Enjoyment: 6/10
Difficulty: 7/10
Would I do it again? Nah, I'm all set.

48. Attend a wine tasting

Why you should try it:
If there's a vineyard near you, visiting it is a great way to support a local business and learn more about wine; if there's not one near you, bringing back a bottle from a vineyard you've visited on vacation is great for reminiscing.

Give it your twist:
- Make your own wine.
- Have a get-together with each guest bringing wine or cheese.
- Share a bottle of wine to celebrate a made-up holiday.

My experience:
I had a perfect Mother's Day: gorgeous weather, a wine tasting and picnic at a local vineyard, and a nice hike with my family. I also cooked a special dinner of beef bourguinon.

And to top it all off, the boys built me a special "momument" in Minecraft.

Enjoyment: 8/10
Difficulty: 1/10
Would I do it again? Yes.

49. Try at least five savory oatmeal recipes

Why you should try it:
Oatmeal is a whole grain that is just as delicious savory as it is sweet. It can be used as a side dish or the centerpiece to a quick, nutritious meal.

Give it your twist:
- Think of your favorite meal; can you replace a carb with oatmeal?
- Try savory ice cream.
- Grill oatmeal like polenta.

My experience:
You are probably already a big fan of sweet oatmeal. These savory oatmeal recipes, though, might just keep you away from those bananas and raisins for a while.

1. Savory oatmeal with fried egg and Parmesan
I kept my first bowl of savory oatmeal simple: Oatmeal with a fried egg and Parmesan. I cooked the oatmeal in vegetable stock and added olive oil, salt, and pepper. Delicious!

2. Mediterranean savory oatmeal
- Oatmeal cooked in vegetable stock
- Sautéed garlic
- Kalamata olives
- Sun-dried tomatoes

- Feta cheese
- Salt and pepper

Delicious. I really liked the olives in it.

3. Curried oatmeal with caramelized onions

First, I made a big batch of caramelized onions. I mixed in curry paste and served it on top of oatmeal cooked in stock.

4. Oatmeal congee

In Thailand, I once had a savory breakfast of jok, a rice porridge called congee in China. It was a bowl of very thin rice, topped with a variety of condiments. For my fourth bowl of savory oatmeal, I used that meal as my inspiration.

One part oatmeal cooked in three parts vegetable stock

Toppings:
- Bean sprouts
- Scallions
- Poached egg
- Ginger
- Garlic
- Cilantro
- Sautéed mushrooms
- Soy sauce
- Lime
- Red pepper flakes

5. Basil pesto oatmeal

I made basil pesto to top my fifth bowl of savory oatmeal.
Ingredients:
- Basil
- Pecorino Romano cheese
- Olive oil
- Pine nuts
- Garlic
- Salt
- Pepper

I topped the oatmeal with the pesto and a little extra olive oil and cheese.

I liked all of these savory oatmeal recipes, but I think my favorite was the first one, with Parmesan cheese, olive oil, and an egg.

Enjoyment: 6/10
Difficulty: 2/10
Would I do it again? Sure, I keep trying new ones.

Link to more savory oatmeal dishes and photos:
http://www.tootimidandsqueamish.com/2011/04/savoring-savory-oatmeal/

50. Take a yoga class again

Why you should try it:
Yoga is great for flexibility, of course, but also for stress relief; laughter yoga was fun to try too.

Give it your twist:
- Try Bikram yoga (hot yoga).
- Do yoga every morning for a month.
- Make a list of 100 awesome moments.

My experience:
"And the forests will echo with laughter.
Does anybody remember laughter?"
– Robert Plant, Led Zeppelin

Supposedly we could laugh in any situation, and we pantomimed laughing while paying the bills, cleaning the house, and talking with a telemarketer.

Laughter lowers stress levels and strengthens the immune system, and the idea behind laughter yoga is that fake laughter is as beneficial as real laughter.

I tend to be leery of anything touchy-feely, so once I heard that laughter yoga has been endorsed by Oprah, Andrew Weil, and Dr. Oz, I was all the more skeptical.

I joined a group of about 40 people, mainly women, and we warmed up with "ha, ha, ha" and "hee, hee, hee." We yukked it up with Santa laughter, silent library laughter, and graduated laughter.

A variety of silly exercises caused some real laughter along with the faking. We all walked around the room and repeatedly paired up for missed high fives. We spoke gibberish to each other, faked angry screaming at each other, and pretended to scare each other.

The biggest real laugh of the class came during the cool down when we were doing deep breathing combined with yawning, and the fake yawns quickly turned to real ones. An elderly gentleman seated in a chair piped up with "I could do this all day."

We had been asked to rate our happiness level at the beginning of the class from one to 10 (with 10 being the best), and I had given myself a 6. I was at an 8 at the end of the session. The funny thing was that I continued to feel an elevated mood for the rest of the day and into the next. That's nothing to laugh at.

I went out for barbecue that night. After my workout, I figured I earned it.

Enjoyment: 8/10
Difficulty: 2/10
Would I do it again? Yes.

51. Tour a Connecticut brewery

Why you should try it:
You will support a local business and probably get free samples.
Give it your twist:
- Go to Oktoberfest.
- Have a Guinness in Ireland.
- Try 5 beers you've never tried.

My experience:
I toured the New England Brewing Co., the brewers of Sea Hag and 668, Neighbor of the Beast, in Woodbridge, CT. While there, I participated in making a batch of beer as well. (See task #54: Brew my own beer.)

Enjoyment:	7/10
Difficulty:	4/10
Would I do it again?	Yes.

52. Go strawberry picking again

Why you should try it:
Picking strawberries in the fresh air is delightful; plus, then you have fresh strawberries.

Give it your twist:
- Pick your own peaches.
- Eat five fruits you've never had before.
- Make strawberry pie.

My experience:
During most trips to my grocery store, I buy fruit and vegetables from thousands of miles away, shipped unripe and picked long ago; they've lost their freshness and a lot of their nutrition sitting on trucks.

By joining a CSA (community supported agriculture), though, I had plenty of opportunities for fresh, local produce and was able to go strawberry picking as well.

Enjoyment: 6/10
Difficulty: 2/10
Would I do it again?   Yes.

53. Eat meatless at least one day a week

Why you should try it:
Going meatless at least once a week can be good for your health, your wallet, and the planet.

Give it your twist:
- Have a meatless potluck dinner and exchange recipes.
- Adapt a favorite meal into a meatless version.
- Get a vegetarian cookbook and try at least 10 new recipes.

My experience:
Meatless Mondays are catching on. Why should you go meatless at least one day a week?

Save the planet
The meat industry is responsible for almost 20 percent of manmade greenhouse gas emissions, as estimated by the United Nations and reported by MeatlessMonday.com. The more people cut down on meat, the less greenhouse gas emissions. Less livestock also means less strain on fresh water and less use of fossil fuel. (If a family of four skips meat and cheese for one day a week for a year, it has the same impact as taking their car off the road for five weeks.)

Improve your health
Most Americans eat more animal protein than is recommended. Too much meat consumption is associated with cancer, cardiovascular disease, and obesity. Many diseases that Americans seem to have started to think of as an inevitable part of aging are not as prevalent in parts of the world that don't eat

the "Western diet" high in animal protein and processed foods. I first became aware of this issue when I read *The China Study*.

Change your mindset

If you do not already eat any vegetarian meals, you may find that taking the opportunity to eat them at least one day a week will cause you to rethink what makes a meal. For example, I always used to picture a hunk of meat, a starch, and a vegetable when I was putting dinner together, but once I had been eating meatless on Mondays for a few months, I began to picture meals differently. When I do serve meat, it is often an accent to the meal, such as some ground turkey in a sauce or a bean-based chili, rather than the centerpiece.

Show some conviction

Why Monday? It doesn't have to be Monday. Any other day would work just as well. On the other hand, by having to abstain on a certain day when you might be presented with a meat-eating situation, you have the opportunity to think about your commitment and follow your convictions. This could also help to …

Spread the word
Make the pledge, and let others know why you're not eating meat. Show them how easy it is.

A Sample Meatless Monday Meal: Quesadilla Casserole

Ingredients:
- 2 sweet potatoes, sliced and roasted
- 2 onions, sliced and sautéed
- 1 red bell pepper, sliced and sautéed
- 1 cup black beans
- 1/2 cup vegetable stock (or water)
- salt and pepper
- 1 cup cheddar cheese, shredded
- 1/2 cup cilantro, chopped
- 1/2 cup enchilada sauce
- 4 whole wheat tortillas

1. Slice and sauté the onions. After about 10 minutes of cooking the onions, add the sliced red bell pepper and cook until tender. Add about half of the black beans. Add a little vegetable stock, and mash the black beans slightly. Add salt and pepper to taste.

2. Mix the remaining half of black beans and the enchilada sauce. Heat through. Mix in the cilantro.

3. Layer the casserole as follows. Tortillas, half of the onion-black bean mixture, half of the sweet potato, half of the cheese, and half of the black bean sauce mixture. Repeat.

4. Bake about 30 minutes at 400 degrees F.

Enjoyment:	7/10
Difficulty:	4/10
Would I do it again?	Yes.

54. Brew my own beer

Why you should try it:
Brewing beer is as old as civilization.

Give it your twist:
- Brew your own hard cider.
- Try a flight of beers at a local microbrewery.
- Make beer cheddar soup.

My experience:
Does goofing off and drinking beer while someone else does all the work count as checking another item off my 101 list? I've been assured that my stirring the brew makes it legitimate.

Enjoyment: 6/10
Difficulty: 4/10
Would I do it again? No.

55. Play, give away, or throw out each of the 32 board games in my basement

Why you should try it:
Unplug from your devices, and break out some old games for some fun interactions around the table.

Give it your twist:
- Organize a board game tournament with adults.
- Invent a board game, and invite friends to play it.
- Have a family game night once a week for 10 weeks in a row.

My experience:
If the evil laugh *mwahahaha* had existed back when my parents were still alive, it would have rung out around the kitchen table whenever someone got set. My mom and dad loved competition. Card games, board games, TV quiz shows: if they could beat you, they would rub it in your face with glee.

When the cards come out these days, I still think of my dad's favorite sayings. "Strong like bull," he'd shout when someone trumped in with a face card. "Let's get 'em out," he'd yell if someone dropped a heart early in a round of "Hearts." He'd ask, "Wait a second — everyone can't make their bid?" with feigned innocence when I was the only one set in a round of "Oh, Heck," and he waited for me to admit, "I got two" on my three-bid.

I gave away most of my towering pile of old board games, but I couldn't let go of "Times to Remember."

When my husband and I were first married, we would visit my parents once a week, and this game was one of our favorites. We'd go couple against couple, young against old.

The game requires you to remember the exact year that something from history happened, so my mom and dad had a slight advantage, having lived through more of it. My mom idolized Elvis, and she and I both remembered her crying on the couch in 1977, when I came home to the news that Elvis had died. Just three years later, it was my turn to cry on the couch at the news that John Lennon had been killed.

On the other hand, being older isn't always an advantage. Sure, the Kennedy assassination or the first man on the moon is easy, but just when was that Cabbage Patch Kids craze? When did the man who played Coach on "Cheers" die? And when did Emperor Hirohito die for that matter? Decades I lived through have become a soup of lumpy mush.

So faced with my board game elimination rule to "use it or lose it," I wanted to save "Times to Remember" and recruited my teenagers to play against my husband and me, young against old.

They were reluctant to play, thinking that they'd be at too big a disadvantage. I reassured them that they're learning these dates in school, while we've had decades to forget them.

Still, we crushed them.

Mwahahaha.

Enjoyment:	6/10
Difficulty:	8/10
Would I do it again?	No, my kids wouldn't let me.

56. Make cheese fondue

Why you should try it:
Gooey goodness and things to dunk: why wouldn't you try it?

Give it your twist:
- Make chocolate fondue.
- Try Chinese fondue.
- Go out for raclette at a Swiss restaurant.

My experience:
We enjoyed cheese fondue by the fire with our eggnog on Christmas Eve. It was worth the effort.

Enjoyment:	8/10
Difficulty:	3/10
Would I do it again?	Yes.

57. Hike Mount Katahdin

Why you should try it:
Hiking is a healthy, inexpensive way to appreciate nature and have fun as a family. Start with a short easy hike, and work your way up to more challenging hikes as you gain experience. (Be sure to bring the proper safety equipment.)

Give it your twist:
- Hike a section of a long trail.
- Arrange to stay in a hut as you complete a multi-day hike.
- Complete a cliff walk.

My experience:
With a grueling 11 hours of continual effort, I managed to complete a project I started with my husband over 20 years earlier: summit all of New England's highest peaks. I may not be a fast hiker, but I am persistent.

My family and I started to hike up Mount Katahdin, Maine's highest peak, at 8 a.m. at the Abol Campground, 3.8 miles from the summit. We hiked pleasantly for a mile or so along Abol Trail, but I slowed down considerably when we reached the boulders and the slide, a tricky area requiring scrambling — using my arms and legs to maneuver and pull myself up and around boulders.

My teenage boys bounded ahead; they waited for my husband and me at the tablelands, a plateau that we reached around 11:30.

From there, it was an easy ascent of one mile to the Katahdin summit, a crowded place on a beautiful August day.

I had found the scramble up to be very challenging and did not want to scramble down it. We took the Appalachian Trail (Hunt Trail) down, a longer route with a gentler grade that turned out to be not so gentle after all.

The scrambles on the Hunt Trail were steep and tricky also, if anything trickier than what we saw on Abol, which made for a mentally and physically challenging 5.2-mile hike down. I didn't finish until 7 p.m., a full three hours later than the average time it takes hikers.

New England's Highest Peaks

Many years earlier, my husband and I did a lot of backpacking, and we set out to summit all of New England's highest peaks. Through a mistake in geography that I don't quite remember, we didn't count Maine as a part of New England, so we never tried Katahdin. Before we knew it, we had kids, and the quest to hike this remote mountain had been tabled for many years. Finally, we were done!

I am so slow and cautious on anything with tricky footing that I doubt I will do another hike this challenging with my speedy kids. I hope they will have many adventures ahead of them going at any pace they please.

Acadia National Park

The day after hiking Katahdin, we visited Acadia National Park. We rested our weary bodies as we traveled by car on the Park Loop Road through the lovely eastern section of Mt. Desert Island. We all felt like cheaters when we stepped out of the car on the summit of Cadillac Mountain. That's not how hikers reach a summit! With blistered feet and aching thighs, though, I gave myself a free pass to enjoy the views.

And the lobster rolls we had were pretty good too.

Enjoyment:	2/10
Difficulty:	10/10
Would I do it again?	No, it's done and I'm done.

58. Go zorbing

Why you should try it:
It was exhilarating to roll down the hill so rapidly on a cushion of air.

Give it your twist:
- Ride a rollercoaster.
- Fly in a blimp.
- Go sailing.

My experience:
"The struggle itself toward the heights is enough to fill a man's heart. One must imagine Sisyphus happy."
– Albert Camus

I've declared repeatedly how empowering it is to face my fears and bask in my newly expanded comfort zone, but I would have liked to skip zorbing.

What is zorbing? Picture a gigantic hamster ball. Insert a woman who is worried she will vomit. Strap her in, and cue the soundtrack: "Oh my God. Oh my God. Oh my God."

Roll her, ass over teakettle, down a bumpy hill.

Driving nearly three hours to reluctantly take a thirty-second ride gave me a lot of time to reflect on whether it's worth it to put myself through the things that I do.

I've always been goal oriented, always pushed or pulled myself a certain way, finding meaning in the struggle. It wasn't fun to put myself through college, several years of hovering near the poverty line with long hours spent hitting the books after working all day, but getting the degree made it worth it, of course.

What about choosing to do stressful things for fun? When I was nearly through my list of completing 101 things in 1001 days, I acknowledged that some of the tasks were of questionable value.

I used to teach Camus' essay "The Myth of Sisyphus." Sisyphus, a character from Greek mythology who defied the gods, endures one of the most terrible punishments they ever doled out. He pushes a massive boulder up a hill, struggling through the pain, to see it roll back down again. Over and over. For eternity. And that's life. We endure misery that accomplishes nothing only to do it again and again. That's quite the message to lay on teenagers in high school English class.

This was all swirling through my mind as my husband and I arrived at the zorbing site. My queasy stomach turned over, and I considered backing out. My husband, who drove me all that way, would not even pretend that was an option.

I nervously got onto a conveyor belt that carried me up the hill. On the way up, I passed a sign — "Caution: Always be aware of other tubers" — and had a vision of an evil Mr. Potato Head attacking me in my zorb.

A staff member opened a creaky gate, and I started rolling down the hill backwards. My world was filled with blue sky, and, a split-second later, green grass. Then blue sky, then green grass, blue sky, green grass, blue, green, blue, green, faster and faster, while I bounced along disoriented on a pillow of air.

Then a guy poked his head in, asking if I was all right. He looked a little sheepish and explained that I really picked up speed in the end, that I won the award for fastest of the day.

I zipped out the hole like it was a playground slide, gasping, "That was crazy."

The twist at the end of Camus' essay is that, with the boulder settled at the foot of the mountain, Camus imagines Sisyphus happy. Life may be absurd, but we control our reactions to it.

So I too am happy when I check each challenge off my list. They're all worth it: the good ones, the bad ones, the silly ones, the profound ones. Sometimes my challenges have taught me something, made me proud, let me share a special moment with the people I love.

And sometimes I'm just glad I didn't vomit.

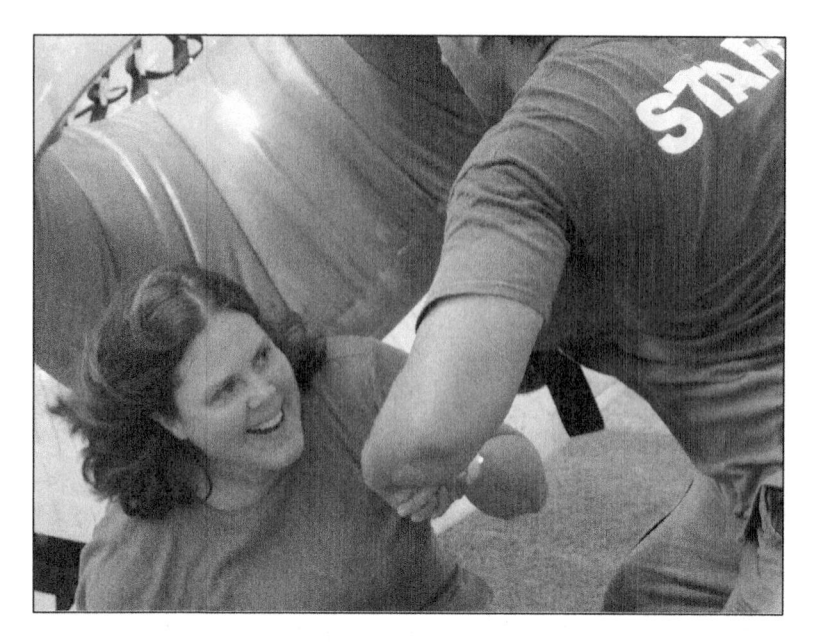

Enjoyment: 7/10
Difficulty: 9/10
Would I do it again? No, no, no!

See the video: http://www.tootimidandsqueamish.com/2013/09/zorbing-gigantic-hamster-ball-meaning-life/

59. Make a wooden frame for the old homemade door panels my dad had made

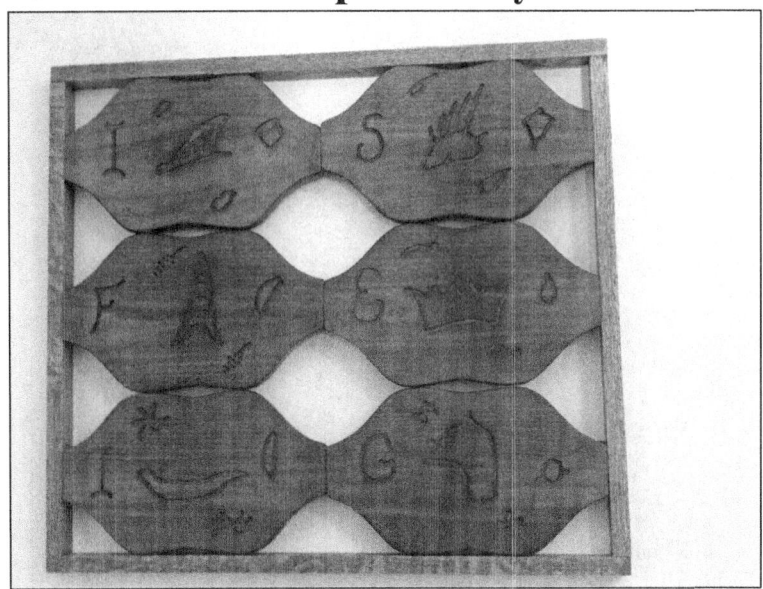

Why you should try it:
Creating something with your hands is so satisfying compared to buying something or paying to have it made. Think of a project that will allow you to display a family heirloom.

Give it your twist:
- Create a custom frame for a special photograph.
- Refinish an old piece of furniture.
- Make a quilt that includes pieces of old clothing.

My experience:
My stubby finger traced the groove's curves, pushing aside the fresh sawdust and smelling its piney scent.

"That's a potato, Marcy," my dad said. "Do you know where they have a lot of potatoes?"

I had no idea.

"In Ireland," he said. "That's where your ancestors came from." While I traced the oval blobs of the potatoes, I heard the motor of his router make the strands of spaghetti for Italy.

I was maybe 5 or 6 and didn't know Irish potatoes from Italian spaghetti, but I did know that I liked to watch my dad work on his machine and learn what all the shapes represented.

My dad created two of each type of six panels, parts of swinging doors in the house of my childhood.

The panels had sat in a dusty heap in my basement for several years, and I finally made a frame for them. Now, as I pause in my writing, stuck on a phrase, my eyes drift along the bagpipe-shaped blob in the frame over my desk.

Scotland, I know.

I made the frame with these steps:

- Lay out the panels and measure the lengths of wood.
- Cut the wood to size on the chop saw. (Loud! Scary!)
- Hammer the four pieces into a frame. Continually get new nails to replace the bent nails.
- Hammer cross beams in place for support. Continually get new nails to replace the bent nails.
- Stain the frame and apply polyurethane.
- Nail the panels into place. Marvel that I showed no improvement in being able to hammer a nail without bending it.

Enjoyment: 7/10
Difficulty: 7/10
Would I do it again?   Yes, and I will hit the nail in straight.

60. Get a pedicure

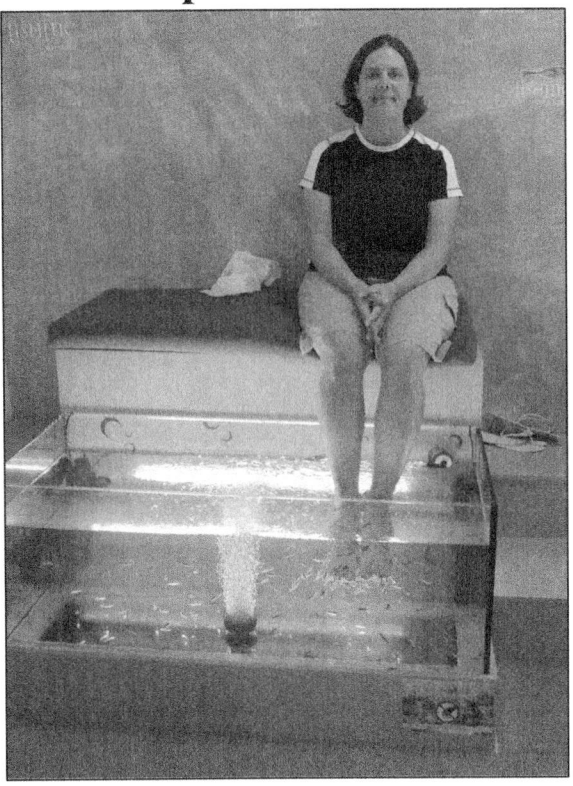

Why you should try it:
Don't let being squeamish keep you from enjoying sensual delights.

Give it your twist:
- Get a massage.
- Schedule a facial.
- Go to a sauna.

My experience:
Having fish nibbling at my toes wasn't the strangest part of the experience when I got a pedicure on Mykonos during my vacation in Greece. By now, I imagine people all over the world have shown a picture of my feet to their curious loved ones.

When I plunged my feet into the cold water, the little Garra Rufa fish immediately started nibbling at the dead skin on my feet. I happened to be sitting at the tank nearest the door, so while I felt timid enough about doing this, it felt extra strange to see the squeamish faces of other tourists coming in and snapping close-ups of my feet.

One woman who looked particularly apprehensive about it asked me, "Is there pain?"

"It kills," I groaned, kidding. Her eyes opened wider. I assured her, though, that it didn't hurt at all. It felt like bubbles from a hot tub were brushing against my feet. After the 15-minute treatment, my feet felt smooth and massaged.

I stayed away from the seafood at dinner that night.

Enjoyment: 6/10
Difficulty: 6/10
Would I do it again? No, once was enough.

61. Have my kids pick five ingredients from the store; feature them in a meal

Why you should try it:
Get your kids involved in the grocery store, and give yourself a cooking challenge.

Give it your twist:
- Have a *Chopped* cooking competition against a friend.
- Make a favorite meal that your grandparent used to make.
- Try to recreate a favorite restaurant meal at home.

My experience:
I vetoed Devil Dogs immediately, but the boys held firm on hot dogs. My sons were given the job to pick out any five ingredients to be included in our dinner. Their choices:
- hot dogs
- elbow macaroni
- escarole
- tomatoes
- Ritz crackers

They could have been a lot more diabolical. There had been talk of caramel, anchovies, and beets as featured ingredients.

I decided to use the hot dogs and escarole in a "Dress it Up, Dress it Down Mac and Cheese." I crisped up hot dog slices, sautéed the escarole, and threw it all together with elbows and a cheese sauce.

I wasn't so sure what to do with the tomatoes and crackers. I finally decided to give the tomatoes a Ritz cracker breading and put them on top.

The verdict: This was one of my more popular family dinners. I wouldn't have planned on the tomato topping, but it worked out well.

At least I didn't have to top the mac and cheese with Devil Dogs. That would have been really diabolical.

Dress it Up, Dress it Down Mac and Cheese

Enjoyment:	7/10
Difficulty:	3/10
Would I do it again?	Yes, I'd like to try a *Chopped*-style competition.

62. Drive a go kart again

Why you should try it:
Racing around a track with the roar of the engine in your ears is thrilling, even in a go kart.

Give it your twist:
- Drive a racecar.
- Go on a helicopter ride.
- Learn to change your own oil.

My experience:
Although I'll get my hackles up if I hear a sexist comment about women drivers, I'll admit it: I'm not a great driver. I have a safe driving record, though, as long as you don't count the time I crashed into my garage while backing out and had to drive to work with my bumper bungeed on. Or the time I crashed into a convenience store that was just sitting there minding its own business while I pulled up at a ripping three miles per hour.

So I was feeling a little insecure about trying high-speed go kart racing at F1 Boston.

It only made matters more scary that two of my brothers were along for the ride. Growing up with them was a series of ultra competitive card games and trivia contests. Yeah, I usually win. It's a lot to live up to, being the best at everything (winky face here for all readers who do not share a significant chunk of my DNA).

My older brother Jay knew I was nervous during our safety orientation, so he peppered in helpful comments like, "Do you think they'll show the crash and burn footage in this video?"

Ready for F1 racing

Geared up in a race suit, helmet, and neck brace, I was sweating and cautious during our first lap under the yellow flag. My nervousness went away instantly as I put the pedal to the metal up the first hill, only to come back seconds later upon seeing the huge "slow" sign before the hairpin turn.

I relaxed a bit and had fun, mainly focusing on just staying out of everyone's way as they passed me like maniacs.

I was lapped several times in the 15-lap race. No worries. There are always card games and trivia contests.

Enjoyment: 7/10
Difficulty: 7/10
Would I do it again? Yes.

63. Go snowshoeing

Why you should try it:
Unlike snowboarding or skiing, you can strap on snowshoes and have success without any experience. It's a great way to get exercise out in the cold.

Give it your twist:
- Make an igloo.
- Create snow angels.
- Have a snowball fight.

My experience:
It was the final winter of my 101 things list, and my husband had talked me out of snowshoeing on one of my only opportunities because there were only a few inches of snow.

"If you can walk through it anyways, it doesn't really count," he argued.

I'm nothing if not a rule follower, even my own self-imposed rules, so I spent several snowless weeks vaguely worrying we wouldn't get enough snow.

Well, we got enough snow. Winter Storm Nemo dropped about 3 feet on Connecticut.

Definitely enough snow.

I traveled across the virgin snow in our backyard pretty well, but my right foot came out a few times, and my leg plunged down, way down, snow up to my thigh.

My husband suggested I check out an abandoned car across the street and make sure no one was stuck inside. I slowly went over and made my way back.

"Did you check in the back seat?" he asked.

"No. What? Why?"

"What if someone is stuck in there in the back seat, waiting for help?"

"There isn't," I said.

"Did you check? What if?"

I knew he was messing with me, but I had to check anyways because *what if?* I strapped them on again and made my way over there. It was all clear.

Enjoyment: 5/10
Difficulty: 4/10
Would I do it again? Yes.

64. Try a new cuisine

Why you should try it:
There are probably some great restaurants right near you that you've never considered going to. You don't have to travel to another country to expand your horizons.

Give it your twist:
- Prepare a three-course meal based on a cuisine you've never cooked.
- Experiment with five new spices.
- Go to a festival celebrating a culture different than your own.

My experience:
The man explained the choices at the steam table, but hesitated at the second pork dish. "And this one is — I don't know if I should tell you what it is." He gave a nervous laugh as he stirred the diced pork in a deep brown sauce.

I was convinced now that it was a rare occurrence that a non-Filipino wandered into his little place, a half restaurant, half Filipino grocery store in Wallingford, CT, called Kayumangi. We assured him it was all right.

I ordered the dish he had been afraid to tell me about, pork in a blood sauce, and he was thrilled, saying, "Wow, you are brave!" There were nods of approval from other customers as well.

My husband and I enjoyed our lunch: two pork dishes, a salted and dried milkfish, and tender little squids, served with white rice.

As we ate, most of the other customers were watching the Filipino television station above our heads, giving me a friendly smile when they caught my eye.

I've done a fair amount of traveling and have often been to restaurants that are quite used to a crush of tourists; it can seem like they are putting on a show. Here, 15 miles from my Connecticut home, I experienced an authentic Filipino meal.

Enjoyment: 7/10
Difficulty: 3/10
Would I do it again? Yes.

65. Get a makeover

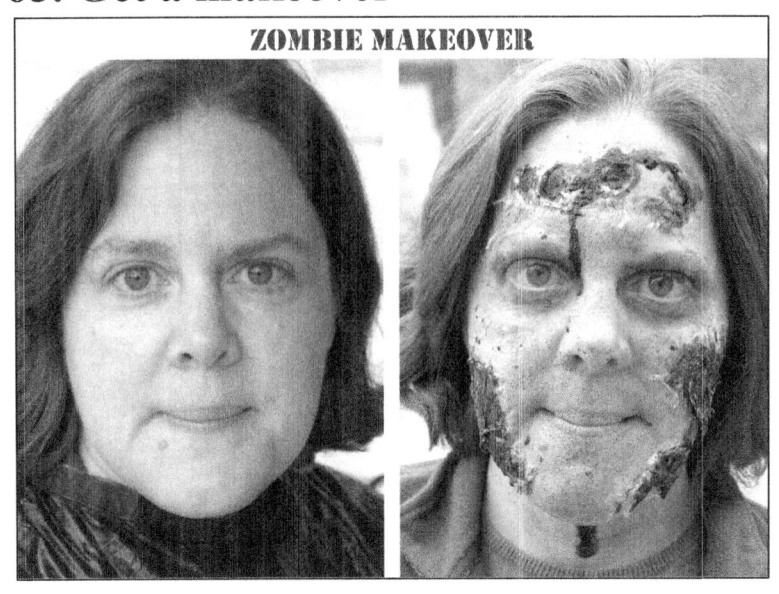

ZOMBIE MAKEOVER

Why you should try it:
Letting a trained expert apply your makeup can teach you the best colors and techniques for yourself. I don't wear makeup, though, so I gave this challenge my own twist.

Give it your twist:
- Meet with a stylist.
- Get a family portrait done.
- Have your eyebrows waxed.

My experience:
Ah, autumn fairs in New England. The leaves are turning, the air is crisp, and the zombies are searching for brains.

Steps to become a zombie:
Step 1: Apply latex.
Step 2: After drying, add some cotton balls to create texture.
Step 3: Create holes for the rotting flesh.
Step 4: Apply accents of color.
Step 5: Apply eye shadow and other shading.
Step 6: Spatter on some blood.
Step 7: Paint on yet more blood.
Step 8: Eat some brains!

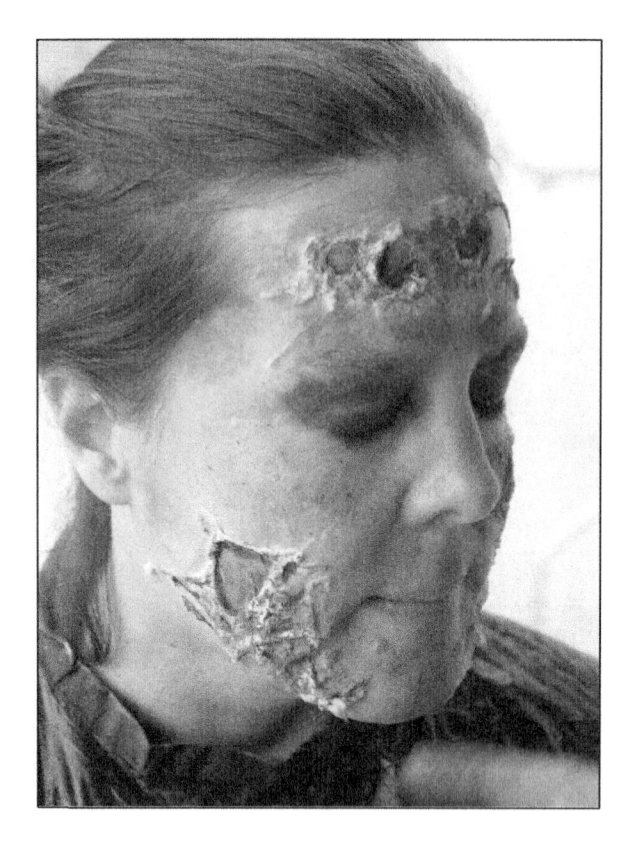

We were at the Doomsday Fair, and the timing was eerie. Hurricane Sandy headed for Connecticut, and local news stations amped up the horror of an October storm one year after the "Storm of the Century" caused record-breaking power outages (and *outrages*) across the state. It was a perfect storm to be afraid, very afraid.

Amid all the craziness was a serious purpose. The fair was organized by the New England Preparedness and Conservation Consortium, a "non-profit organization dedicated to conservation of our natural resources, sustainability of our natural environment, and to helping people learn to harness the strengths of our natural elements to become more self reliant" (NEPACC).

Six things I learned about zombies:

You can really learn a lot about zombies by walking a mile in their shoes.

1. Zombies just want to have fun.
2. Zombies need a little TLC.
3. Zombies enjoy a peaceful stroll along the Connecticut River. (The funniest part of my day was seeing the reactions of passersby who didn't know about the fair.)
4. Zombies should wear their seat belts.
5. Even zombies need a friend.

6. After a long day, zombies just want to relax on the couch with a glass of wine.

But they have to go down in their basements and check on the flashlights and the MREs.

Enjoyment: 7/10
Difficulty: 3/10
Would I do it again? Probably not.

See more zombie photos:
http://www.tootimidandsqueamish.com/2012/10/apocalypse-soon-i-become-a-zombie-at-the-doomsday-fair/

66. Write a haiku each day for a week that sums up or reflects upon the day

Sunday in the fall
Blankets, couch, and Breaking Bad
Oh, hibernation

Why you should try it:
Capturing the essence of your day in 17 syllables is a thought-provoking challenge.

Give it your twist:
- Do the same thing, but with a limerick a day.
- Complete a photo-a-day challenge (for a month? For a year?)
- Send a different friend a letter each day for a week.

My experience:
My one-o-one list
Has a task to write haiku
Each day for a week

Sunday:
Sunday in the fall
Blankets, couch, and *Breaking Bad*
Oh, hibernation

Monday:
Field trip to high ropes
Scared kids and I wait to zip
I feel twelve again

Tuesday:

Son's meet in the park
Crunching leaves under his feet
"Run, Dan, run," I cheer

Wednesday:
I must grade a quiz
Teach of hunter-gatherers
Rush to a meeting

Thursday:
Not much happening
Work, then chores, then cook dinner
A pretty good day

Friday:
Out for drinks with friends
Good times around the table
Crush at setback too

Saturday:

Took a curling class
Sweep, sweep, so the stone goes straight
I will sweep with you

Enjoyment: 5/10
Difficulty: 4/10
Would I do it again?   Probably not.

67. Go to at least five offbeat or small museums

Why you should try it:
There are probably some great museums nearby that you've never even heard about. Avoid the crowds and learn something new by going to some small museums.

Give it your twist:
- Google "offbeat museums" in your area to learn what's around.
- Companies with long histories often have historical exhibits.
- Visit a historical house in your town.

My experience:
I learned the trick to getting my teenage son to come along to the Pez Museum with me: Promise him a bucket of candy.

Well, how did I get my husband to come along to the Trash Museum with me?

Promise him a bucket of beer.

First, we searched for scavenger hunt items in the Temple of Trash. Note the seagull eerily poised above my family's heads, a perfect reminder of childhood trips to the dump.

So that's where all those unwanted America Online discs ended up?

The museum, run by the Connecticut Resources Recovery Authority, was well organized with information on recycling and reducing waste.

After touring the exhibits, we watched the trucks coming in and the recyclables being sorted from the mountain of debris.

Museum trip finished, we moved on to the rest of our afternoon, lunch at City Steam, a brew house and restaurant.

We picked up growlers for a haggis feast planned later that night, another task from my 101 things list.

As we approached our car in the parking garage, we heard a woman shout to us: "Anyone want to help me get a dead bird off my car?"

This was either the weirdest set up to a mugging or a woman who needed help getting a dead bird off her car.

My husband said the only thing he could say in that situation: "Sure!"

He went over to her car expecting a little robin or sparrow, and there was a humongous seagull, dead, with its leg stuck in her headlight. She had been standing there for who knows how long, trying to pull it out and losing her nerve.

Bird removed, it was time for us to go home and prepare the haggis.

Enjoyment:	5/10
Difficulty:	1/10
Would I do it again?	For different ones, yes.

68. Get a graphic that represents my blog, "(Don't Be) Too Timid and Squeamish"

Why you should try it:
What images would you choose to represent your life? Make a collage.
Give it your twist:
- Decorate something with needlepoint.
- Write your name in calligraphy.
- Photoshop your head on a superhero's body.

My experience:
I made a header for my blog.

Enjoyment: 5/10
Difficulty: 2/10
Would I do it again? Yes.

69. Visit at least three "Road Food" places I have never been to

Why you should try it:
There are probably many beloved and inexpensive places to get a quick bite all around you. Check some of them out.

Give it your twist:
- Try a progressive dinner road trip: get an appetizer at one place.
- Get a main course at the next stop.
- Have dessert at the final place.

My Experience:
After I completed the Connecticut Hot Dog Tour, it was safe to say I wouldn't be eating another hot dog anytime soon.

A group of men, including my husband, organized a tour of 10 famed hot dog joints in the state (a bonus eleventh one was thrown in spontaneously). These guys don't mess around. They had an official tee shirt and soundtrack, and we traveled in style on a party bus. And we had hot dogs. Lots of hot dogs.

A woman on the tour agreed to split dogs with me. Most of the men ate all of the full dogs, with some "tapping out" when they needed to.

1. Rawley's Drive-In, Fairfield
The Order: Works, with "mustard, relish, kraut, and bacon," $3.00.

The Verdict: Delicious dog, with a good contrast between the tangy kraut and the crunchy bacon. This was a great start to the tour.

2. Super Duper Weenie, Fairfield

The Order: Georgia Redhot, a "1/4 lb. spicy Southern sausage with sauerkraut, mustard and our own sweet relish," $4.25.

The Verdict: This big boy was delicious too. The sausage was split and grilled and served piping hot with excellent toppings. We were on a roll.

3. Danny's Drive-In, Stratford

People insisted we had to try Danny's nearby, and it was inserted into our tour.

The Order: Bull Dog, with "spicy chili and fried onions," $3.95.

The Verdict: I liked this all right at the time, but I soon started worrying about the spicy chili not sitting so well with a long day of half-dogs ahead. The group's mood lagged on the way to the next stop. The consensus seemed to be that we should not have inserted this extra dog into the tour.

4. Glenwood Drive-In, Hamden

The Order: Hot dog, with mustard and hot relish put on at the counter, $3.95.

The Verdict: This was the winner of the day, an excellent charbroiled dog with a toasted bun and great hot relish. Many people on the tour voted this one the winner.

5. Top Dog, Portland

The Order: Orleans Dog, with "a hot and sweet relish," $2.70.

The Verdict: My husband, a Portland native, tried to warn the tour against this stop. It was not a favorite. The owners were very sweet and friendly, and you can't beat the décor, so that almost made it worth a visit.

6. Doogie's, Newington

The Order: The Doogie Dog, "One of my Best Ever Creations. Caramelized Onions & Dijon Horsey Sauce," $3.59.

The Verdict: A nicely charred, delicious dog, and the toppings were a refreshing change after having a lot of spicy chilies and relishes. One member of the tour ordered — and put away — a two-foot dog.

Interlude in the Park

We were all greatly restored by a visit to Stanley Quarter Park in New Britain and a walk around the pond.

7. Capitol Lunch, New Britain

The Order: Hot dog, with "mustard, onions, sauce," $1.75.

The Verdict: I liked it, and I remembered it fondly from my college days. The group, though, seemed unnerved by its strangely black sauce. And I didn't remember it looking like that.

8. Blackie's, Cheshire

The Order: Hot dog, with corn relish and mustard at the counter, $1.75.

The Verdict: I had been here before and had liked its famous relish. It didn't disappoint.

9. Frankie's, Waterbury

The Order: Hot dog, "French with spicy cheddar cheese," $3.49.

The Verdict: Nice dog, nice sauce. This was a tasty hot dog, and there were a lot more varieties that looked promising. This late in the day, though, people sort of slouched when they saw the size of it.

10. Al's Hot Dogs, Naugatuck

The Order: Hippo Dog, "cheese, chili, kraut, bacon," $4.49.

The Verdict: Pretty good, but enough, already. I think this bad boy would have been more appreciated earlier in the day.

11. Merritt Canteen, Bridgeport

The Order: Brutal Dog, "Georgia Red Hot with Chili," $4.00.

The Verdict: This was so hot, so spicy, such a brutal end to the night. I suspect it was good, but my lips were burning too much to tell.

End of the Night

This was a great tour with a great group of people. The men had a much tougher time than the women, who were splitting dogs. This end of the night quote by one of the men summed it up well at the last stop: "Don't touch me!" On the way home, he explained: "I feel like E.T. at the end of the movie when he was all gray and his heart was fading."

As for me, I'll be going vegetarian for a while.

Enjoyment:	6/10
Difficulty:	7/10
Would I do it again?	Not in one day!

70. Eat haggis

Why you should try it:
I have never been one for "weird food" challenges, but there are many traditional meals that are worth a try. Is there anything you are curious to try?

Give it your twist:
- Try Rocky Mountain "oysters." (They're not oysters.)
- Have oxtail soup.
- Eat Jamaican jerked goat.

My experience:
In the remote Scottish highlands walks a weirdly evolved creature, the wild haggis, whose legs are longer on one side of his body to help him navigate the steep hills of his homeland.

That's not true, of course. One survey, though, found that a third of American visitors to Scotland believed that the wild haggis was a real creature.

Aye, ya bampot.

Haggis, a Scottish traditional dish, does not immediately make me think, "I want to eat some of that." Sheep's heart, liver, and lungs are combined with oatmeal and spices to make a savory pudding that is stuffed into a sheep's stomach.

Does this offal sound awful?

I have always been curious to try haggis, and it was actually pretty good, with a rich savory flavor and a creamy texture. A few bites of it, though, were plenty to satisfy both my curiosity and my appetite.

Along with the haggis, I served some other Scottish delicacies: potato scones, black pudding, mushy peas, and a Scotch egg (a hard-boiled egg encased in sausage and baked).

The scones and mushy peas were delicious, the egg was pretty good, and I could have done without the black pudding. I ordered the food fully cooked from a Scottish market in New Jersey and just had to heat everything.

And what kind of bevvy should be served alongside our haggis feast? Scotch, of course. According to the men, the Scotch was great. I nursed mine along, not appreciating it.

All in all, it was a fun night, and I enjoyed trying haggis for the first time.

Slàinte mhath!

Enjoyment: 5/10
Difficulty: 3/10
Would I do it again? I would if I went to Scotland.

71. Try to grow sunflowers again

Why you should try it:
Sunflowers are gorgeous and cheery, and if you get to harvest the seeds, that's all the better.

Give it your twist:
- Grow roses.
- Keep bees.
- Make chocolate covered sunflower seeds.

My experience:
"If a plant cannot live according to its nature, it dies; and so a man."
– Henry David Thoreau

I had called myself out a few months earlier for not giving an earnest effort to grow sunflowers even though I had checked the task off my list. So as the temperature plunged, I borrowed a grow light and set up some small self-watering containers down in my basement. Sure enough, within a week or so life sprang forth, with the little sprouts pushing their seed coverings up through the soil and wearing them like silly hats.

I started with about 30 sprouts. They quickly outgrew their plastic containers, and I transferred the biggest to some pots. Another month, another transfer, until I had six big plants. About once a week, the plants grew up to the light, and I had to raise the platform.

I always get a little down in the winter as the days get shorter and the cold keeps me indoors, but I got a lift each day when I went down to the basement to water the plants and saw that they'd grown bigger since my last visit.

While the polar vortex swirled outside my Connecticut window, little triangles pushed forth from the center of the biggest plant. A bud was swelling, and inside that whirl of shapes, a flower was waiting to emerge.

My husband, a biology teacher, cautioned that plants may not flower if conditions are not right, that they'll conserve their energy instead. Nevertheless, a flower bloomed.

Enjoyment:	6/10
Difficulty:	5/10
Would I do it again?	Yes.

72. Go through the basement bins and donate, sell, or throw out what I can

Why you should try it:
If a year or two has gone by without unboxing something after a move, you could probably get rid of it.

Give it your twist:
- Donate the clothes you no longer wear.
- Get rid of one thing each day for 60 days in a row.
- Set up a basement worm farm.

My experience:
See #47: Jump off a cliff.

Enjoyment: 2/10
Difficulty: 7/10
Would I do it again? If needed.

73. Knit something

Why you should try it:
Making something with your hands to give to someone else is so charming.

Give it your twist:
- Make mittens.
- Make a stuffed animal.
- Make potholders.

My experience:
From a year earlier: I am not schooled in the domestic arts, nor am I coordinated. I needed to take to YouTube to see how to knit when I couldn't decipher written directions, and then I had to specially find left-handed directions because it was the shame of high school tennis all over again when I tried to convert the right-handed view in my head and failed.

Somehow my husband, who was watching football in the other room and barely paying attention, knew I should make a ball of yarn rather than use the skein, and I watched a video to see the best way to do that. The little ball jumped out of my hand several times, causing me to curse and spill my coffee. The skein on the floor unrolled reluctantly in fits and jerks like a fish fighting on a line.

I cast stitches on my needle for a scarf, though. That was enough for day number one.

From three months earlier: I had abandoned that previous effort when the stitches inexplicably got tighter and tighter until I couldn't move the needles.

Since time was ticking down on my 101 things list, I mentioned at work that I was considering taking a knitting class. Someone said she could show me how. We decided that I would do it right-handed because that's how she knew to show me, and after ten minutes I was on my way.

From two months earlier: I plugged away at my little pattern of yarn while my husband watched the Red Sox in the World Series. I occasionally paid attention to those bearded boys of Boston.

From the last month: The men on the field changed their baseballs for footballs, and my creation stretched out before me and eventually could reach over my head. I surprised myself by enjoying knitting, the perfect fall activity while curled up on the couch with my husband.

And he sure looks good in that scarf, doesn't he?

Enjoyment:	7/10
Difficulty:	7/10
Would I do it again?	Yes.

74. Make butter

Why you should try it:
It's so much fun to try your hand at making a simple food from scratch, and you avoid all the chemicals that are routinely pumped into your food.

Give it your twist:
- Make homemade bread.
- Make homemade ricotta cheese.
- Make homemade mayonnaise.

My experience:
Feeling like I was in the middle of a Shake Weight infomercial, I took my turn shaking the heavy cream to make homemade butter.

To make about a half cup of butter, first I measured out a cup of heavy cream.

After a few minutes of shaking, it had thickened quite a bit. It was thicker still after more shaking. And more shaking.

It got very thick and hard to shake. Then, it got easy to shake again as the buttermilk separated from the butter and sloshed around free in the container.

I poured off the buttermilk. This can be used in other recipes, such as biscuits and pancakes.

It took about 15 minutes to turn the cream into butter. I stirred in a pinch of salt, and we had some on toast. It was creamy and delicious (as butter always is). We had some the next day on homemade bread.

Enjoyment: 5/10
Difficulty: 1/10
Would I do it again? Probably not, but it was fun to try.

75. Read at least 15 classics I've never read

Why you should try it:
Reading the classics opens you up to other cultures and time periods. It also teaches you about yourself.

Give it your twist:
- Read three books of types that you don't usually choose.
- Go to three book club meetings.
- Read a book about the history of a place you plan to travel to.

My experience:
I despised the beginning of the novel *Rebecca*, a tedious, drawn-out slog through the ruins of an English estate. And I felt scorn for the narrator, too, a fearful lower-class woman who married up and hid from the servants so they wouldn't catch her behaving inappropriately. She constantly felt she didn't measure up to her husband's first wife, Rebecca, a beautiful, fearless woman.

I wanted to shout at her: "Suck it up, girl! Just stop worrying about every little thing!"

Then about page 144, it hit me. She is just like I am.

The narration that was getting on my nerves could have come from inside my own head (if I lived on an upper-class country estate surrounded by servants), double guessing myself and being uncertain about every little thing, being timid (and squeamish, too).

Here, the narrator tries to explain to her husband why she hates visiting people, a social obligation she is forcing herself through:

"'I try every day, every time I go out or meet anyone new. I'm always making efforts. You don't understand. It's all very well for you, you're used to that sort of thing. I've not been brought up to it.'

"'Rot,' said Maxim, 'it's not a question of bringing up, as you put it. It's a matter of application. You don't think I like calling on people, do you? It bores me stiff. But it has to be done, in this part of the world.'

"'We're not talking about boredom,' I said, 'there's nothing to be afraid of in being bored. If I was just bored it would be different. I hate people looking me up and down as though I were a prize cow.'

"'Who looks you up and down?'

"'All the people down here. Everybody.'

"'What does it matter if they do? It gives them some interest in life.'

"'Why must I be the one to supply the interest, and have all the criticism?'

"'Because life at Manderlay is the only thing that ever interests anybody down here.'

"'What a slap in the eye I must be to them then.'"

It was exciting later in the book when she grew some *cojones* and started talking back.

Since I started my blog, I have been working to get out of my comfort zone. My internal monologue has changed some for the better. Why should I feel fearful about walking into a room? I know I shouldn't, and yet...

As for getting out of my comfort zone, I see that it's not really a matter of getting out of my comfort zone, but of expanding the boundaries bit by bit so that I have a little more breathing room.

For the rest of *Rebecca*, I was hooked.

Enjoyment:	6/10
Difficulty:	6/10
Would I do it again?	Yes, so many great books.

76. Eat a cheeseburger at Louis' Lunch

Why you should try it:
Look into any historical food firsts in your area, and visit the restaurants.

Give it your twist:
- Visit a restaurant that your parents or grandparents loved.
- Go to a nearby city and eat at a historic landmark.
- Revisit a restaurant that you loved as a child.

My experience:
We squeezed into the crowd of wall-to-wall people to wait our turn to eat a hamburger at Louis' Lunch in New Haven, CT. Reportedly, the American hamburger was invented here in 1900 when a man in a hurry rushed in and asked for a meal he could eat quickly, and Louis Lassen threw a broiled beef patty between two slices of bread for him to eat on the go.

The wait is quite a bit longer now, as Louis' Lunch has become a Connecticut landmark. My husband and I had potato salad while we waited and were lucky to get one of the tiny adorable booths that seat one person on each side.

The atmosphere of the place was very friendly, with the waitresses joking with the cook and the customers. The wait was about an hour — very long for 3 p.m. on a Saturday — but it seemed much faster for the regulars who were fit in between the other orders.

The burgers are made from beef that is ground fresh daily and broiled vertically on both sides at once in a cast iron grill.

The burgers were juicy and tasty. They are served on toast, and the only garnishes allowed are cheese, onion, and tomato. No ketchup; no mustard; no pickles!

"Hold the pickles, hold the lettuce…"

> THIS IS NOT
> **BURGER KING**
> YOU DON'T GET IT YOUR WAY.
> YOU TAKE IT MY WAY,
> OR YOU DON'T GET
> THE DAMN THING.

Enjoyment: 6/10
Difficulty: 1/10
Would I do it again? Sure.

77. Make my own hummus

Why you should try it:
Hummus is a perfect, easy appetizer to serve to guests or bring to a party.

Give it your twist:
- Make baklava.
- Cook your own caramel.
- Ferment your own vinegar.

My experience:
It was easy and tasty to make my own hummus.

I combined chickpeas, tahini, garlic, lemon, salt, pepper, and hot sauce in a food processor until smooth. I added a little olive oil and paprika to the top.

It was better and cheaper than what I can pick up in the grocery store.

Enjoyment:	6/10
Difficulty:	1/10
Would I do it again?	Yes, so easy and good.

78. Finalize my will

LIVING WILL

A. If I have been diagnosed by following are true:
- I have an incurable and irreversible con[dition]
- I have death within a relatively short ti[me]
- administration of life-sustaining treat[ment]
- I am in an irreversible coma
- I am in a persistent vegetative s[tate]
- I am no longer able to make decisions
- I willfully and voluntarily ma[ke]
- ...ficial life support sys[tem]
- ...withdraw tre[atment]

Why you should try it:
Making your will can be difficult to think about, but you'll be glad to get your affairs in order.

Give it your twist:
- Become an organ donor.
- Learn to meditate.
- Set up a scholarship fund.

My experience:
"When Chekhov saw the long winter, he saw a winter bleak and dark and bereft of hope. Yet we know that winter is just another step in the cycle of life. But standing here among the people of Punxsutawney and basking in the warmth of their hearths and hearts, I couldn't imagine a better fate than a long and lustrous winter."

–Phil, *Groundhog Day*

I love the scene in *Groundhog Day* when Phil, after clowning through his life for so long, finally gets it right. His tribute to the day that he was cursed to live over and over again brings a round of applause.

I put off the one item on my bucket list that actually involved my kicking the bucket for a long, long time. On the occasion of finalizing both my will and my living will I felt like I needed to come up with something profound to say, and I kept thinking of Phil's remarks about winter. I find, though, that all

I feel is that it's about time I stopped procrastinating and became a full-fledged grown up, which is what having a will represents to me.

Now, if I am in a persistent vegetative state, people will know what to do, and if my husband and I were both to die at the same time, it would be clear what our wishes are.

(Knock wood.)

I'd like to think Phil would approve.

Enjoyment:	1/10
Difficulty:	5/10
Would I do it again?	No, won't need to.

79. Dance my way through Dance Central with Kinect

Why you should try it:
The minutes fly by when you're dancing without even noticing you're exercising, or at least that's what people who know how to dance tell me.

Give it your twist:
- Participate in a dance marathon.
- Make a ship in a bottle.
- Throw a pot on a wheel.

My experience:
"I can't get no satisfaction."
— The Rolling Stones

I've never been accused of busting a move, but I've learned yet again that persistence pays off.

About two years ago, I started playing the Dance Central game for Xbox's Kinect. At first I thought Kinect was amazing, as my whole body became the controller. What was cool about it, though, quickly became my downfall. That one-eyed snob knew I wasn't *Stylin'* correctly and wouldn't let me advance.

Early in the game, I could handle Lady Gaga's "Poker Face" with its easy *Step Side and Clap* move. Hell, that move got me through the 80s. I could even manage *Love Warrior* and *Headwrush* on another song, but if any kids had been present, they would have posted it to YouTube. And not in a good way.

After the beginner levels, I hit a wall and failed dance routines repeatedly. It turned out that my years of only dancing after cocktails if "Brown Eyed Girl" came on did nothing to prepare me for this challenge. When it comes to dance moves like *West Hop* and *Bring It*, "Hella good," I'm not.

I'm a rock and roll girl at heart, and dancing to the likes of Bell Biv DeVoe or Wreckx-N-Effect just doesn't come naturally to me.

The final straw came when my older son, who was totally uninterested in dancing and had to be bribed to play the game with me, was able to shake his booty easily enough to pass the songs on his first try. And compared to me he has hardly any booty to shake.

I had to finish the game since it's on my list, so I naturally avoided playing it for two solid years.

With my deadline looming, however, the cartoon dancers and I finally reached an understanding. I would work on it 20 minutes a day, every day, repeating the songs until I earned at least three stars. I know I'll never pull off a hip *Snap Walk*, but I rocked the *All Y'All*. And I totally nailed the *Nerd It Out*. Go figure.

The game's "break it down" mode taught me the moves in slow motion. That's when the cartoon dancers had to step up the empathy, telling me, "It's tricky, I know, but you got it." And when that didn't produce the results they were looking for, they'd mutter a vague "Maybe with some more work…" before going on to the next move.

I did eventually make progress, mirroring the dancers like a trained bear.

For full disclosure, I'll point out that it shouldn't be hard to get at least three stars on the easy level. I didn't realize exactly how easy it should have been until I sat down on the couch to take some notes for writing this and earned one star without doing any dancing, the exact score I received when I was dancing. That's just cold.

Once I made it through all the songs, I realized I needed at least four stars on each in order to unlock all the challenges. By then it was no problem. I had learned how to drop it like it's hot.

I will never be "Ace of the Asphalt," but I found I could get some satisfaction from finishing this game. I owe apologies to my rock and roll peeps, though. I've caught myself singing Wreckx-N-Effect's "Rump Shaker" at odd moments:

"All I wanna do is zoom a zoom zoom zoom
And a poom poom, just shake ya rump."

Enjoyment:	7/10
Difficulty:	9/10
Would I do it again?	Maybe — it was fun, though frustrating.

80. Complete at least one other athletic challenge

Why you should try it:
There are so many different choices now for mud runs or obstacle courses, and signing up with a group will make the training fun.

Give it your twist:
- Take a self-defense class.
- Run through a sprinkler with your clothes on (or off?)
- Learn to ride a unicycle.

My experience:
Crawling in mud on my hands and knees while ducking under barbed wire on a chilly Massachusetts morning isn't usually my idea of fun, but it turned out to be a blast.

I had been hemming and hawing about signing up for the Rugged Maniac 5K Obstacle Race for months, especially since the other women on my team dropped out. I prepared and got to the point where I felt confident enough about the running, but the obstacles — huge walls, tunnels, cold water pits — were something that I didn't know whether I could do on my own.

Our team, "Fifty Shades of Mud," ended up being just five of us: my husband Randy, my two teenage boys, my husband's friend Jordan, and I. I planned to let the boys and men run ahead at their own paces and go at my slower pace, and that is what we did.

I had some occasional stabs of loneliness when I saw teams helping each other over certain challenging obstacles, but one thing I didn't anticipate was how empowering it would be to get over, under, and through all the obstacles on my own. Especially those dreaded walls!

I did hold hands with one woman to navigate the pilings, tall columns that were about five feet apart that we had to jump along. She was a woman I had chatted with before the start who was also on her own, so it was nice to have a hand when I really needed one.

Rugged Maniac Race Report

We lined up for our 10:45 start time at about 10:30. The first obstacle didn't even count as part of the race, a plywood barrier about four feet tall that I needed to climb over.

Eying it made me nervous before the race even started, but when I got over it with no problem, I felt a little burst of confidence.

It was a fun atmosphere in the waiting area, with people stretching, hopping, joking, basically a lot of visibly nervous people killing time. A lot of teams dressed up in cool costumes. Tutus were particularly popular. I loved the man in the gilded Roman toga, and we saw a team in business suits and ties. (I wish I saw them crawling through the mud.)

The announcer shouted, "Rugged!," and we yelled, "Maniac!" a couple of times, and then we were off.

My two teenage boys shot ahead, then Jordan, then Randy, then me. I settled into a pretty good pace (for slow me) and held it until I came to the first obstacle, a stepped wall of about 13 feet to climb up and over. I did fine on that one, but was a little freaked going over the top.

My hardest obstacles came next: two separate 7-foot walls to get over (height estimated). Thankfully, there was a little lip of wood to step on, and I then reached with my arms to pull myself up to standing, flung a leg over, and painfully scraped the rest of me over. I was worried about dropping down the full height on the other side, and I bruised my hands and arms trying to hold on while I lowered myself. On the second one, my technique was a little better, and I didn't get any new bruises. Those obstacles were my most dreaded, so I felt really good getting over them and running ahead.

The rest of the race is a jumble in my mind, but these were some of the obstacles:

- Crawling in mud under barbed wire (actually kind of fun, but very cold, and I really didn't appreciate the rocks)
- Crouching through an underground tunnel (I was in pitch black darkness for about 8 seconds of it; freaky)
- Jumping into water pits and climbing out the other side (cold, and seemingly increasingly colder as the course progressed)
- Swimming over or under floating barriers in a muddy water pool (I went over; I was really cold by then)
- Climbing up through a watery, muddy tunnel with the help of a knotted rope (challenging)

- Sliding down a gigantic slide into a pool of chilly water (bashed into people in front of me and got bashed by those behind me, and this was supposed to be the fun one!)
- Running over fire (looked badass, but not a problem)
- Hills, hills, and hills, up and down a Motocross course (ugh, I admit to walking the steep, muddy hills)
- Rolling across an elevated cargo net (this was the last obstacle; I could have put up with anything by that point)

One perk of being slower than the rest of my team? My husband was able to get our camera back and cheer me on for my finish.

After the race, we got cleaned up with the milk jugs of water we had stashed in the car (avoiding the freezing hoses) and returned for our complimentary beer from Harpoon Brewery. Now we're talking. We ate and walked around, soaking up the scene.

I am very glad to have checked this off my list, so to speak. It was fun, but I can't tell you how glad I was that it was over. I had been worrying about this race for months.

And now I can finally say: "I'm a rugged maniac!"

Enjoyment: 6/10
Difficulty: 8/10
Would I do it again? Probably not.

81. Cook something with tofu or tempeh

Why you should try it:
Tofu and tempeh are easy ways to add protein to a meatless dish.

Give it your twist:
- Make ratatouille.
- Cook curry from scratch.
- Bake crème brûlée.

My experience:
I am not a big fan of tofu, but the stir-fry I made was tasty.

Enjoyment:	3/10
Difficulty:	3/10
Would I do it again?	Yes.

82. Visit at least five "Roadside America" attractions

Why you should try it:
There are so many fun places on the side of the road. Taking a few minutes to check them out can bring a lot of inexpensive fun, and you'll appreciate them more every time you drive by them.

Give it your twist:
- Check out the "Roadside America" attractions during your next road trip.
- Research the stories behind the places in your town.
- Make a photo collage of your town's quirky claims to fame.

My experience:
A fun day of road tripping lay ahead when I picked out five "Roadside America" attractions to check out in my area. My husband was a good sport as we traveled around in between going out to eat and getting errands done.

First up: the Paul Bunyan Muffler Man
I have driven by him many times. He was in good shape without a flag. He seemed even bigger up close than he does from the road.

Second stop: the Wheel Auto Parts Man

Such a friendly bloke.

Third attraction: the Barker Character, Comic and Cartoon Museum

We toured the grounds, the art gallery, and the museum, which was chock full of character toys and artifacts, everything from an old metal lunchbox collection to a model for filming Gumby animation. This brought back a lot of old memories — "Welcome Back, Kotter," "Alfred E. Newman," old cardboard single serving cereal boxes, push button puppets; all the bits of my childhood that I didn't save are gathered in one place. They had new items too. The strangest thing that caught my eye was the President Obama CelebriDuck, grouped with some other CelebriDucks. Why?

Fourth attraction: Wild Bill's Nostalgia Center

This wildly decorated junk shop also features the world's largest Jack-in-the-Box, so it's got that going for it. It was fun to browse through the old concert posters and memorabilia.

We then went down to New Haven for a cheeseburger at Louis' Lunch, another Roadside America attraction.

Fifth attraction: world's largest mobile crane

We went to Wooster Square Park in New Haven to check out the Jesus Tree, a site where a young woman's claim to have seen an apparition of Jesus in 1992 attracted some attention. It was supposed to be a sycamore in the Southwestern quadrant of the park. There were two sycamores that were possibilities, and they both had had some limbs removed since then. (Does that seem wrong?) We were freezing in a windy drizzle and snapped a couple of pictures and fled.

We didn't think this quite qualified as a fifth attraction, so we made a change in plans and decided to fit in one more site before stopping in on a Middletown pub. This twist of fate allowed us to witness the world's largest mobile crane!

Enjoyment:	8/10
Difficulty:	3/10
Would I do it again?	Sure, I like offbeat places.

83. Have a cookout again

Why you should try it:
Somehow burgers taste better in the backyard.

Give it your twist:
- Have a New England clam bake.
- Throw a luau themed party.
- Set up a taco bar for dinner.

My experience:
I like having cookouts, but it's one of those things we never seem to get around to doing. It's really not so hard to carry some plates and buns to the backyard.

Enjoyment: 7/10
Difficulty: 3/10
Would I do it again? Yes.

84. Make my own nut butter

Why you should try it:
A lot of commercial peanut butters are filled with junk; it's easy to make your own nut butter.

Give it your twist:
- Create your own fortune cookies.
- Make homemade tortillas.
- Cook your own ketchup.

My experience:
This simple nut butter is so easy to make and so special to have on my morning oatmeal.

Maple Macadamia Nut Butter
Ingredients:
8 oz. raw macadamia nuts
2 teaspoons maple syrup
pinch salt

Mix the ingredients together in a food processor until a smooth butter forms (about 10 minutes), scraping down occasionally.

I had the macadamia nuts left over from when I made vegan cake pops. The nut butter was perfect as a topping for oatmeal.

Back to School Oatmeal

1/2 cup oats
1/2 cup unsweetened almond milk
1 tablespoon maple macadamia nut butter
1 teaspoon raisins
1 teaspoon pepitas (shelled pumpkin seeds)
dash cinnamon

I like the touch of sweetness that the nut butter gives, since I used unsweetened almond milk.

Enjoyment:	6/10
Difficulty:	2/10
Would I do it again?	Yes.

85. Hit a bucket of golf balls again

Why you should try it:
Empty your mind and focus on only your swing; if the ball's not still on the tee when you're done, count it as a success.

Give it your twist:
- Go fly a kite.
- Try trampolining.
- Solve a Rubik's Cube.

My experience:
I hit a bucket of golf balls on a beautiful spring afternoon, and at least a few of them went far, straight, and true. I looked up in time to see them arcing gracefully against the blue sky and puffy white clouds.

Most of them, though, went puttering off the tee or awkwardly left or right. I took to proclaiming "Shanked it!" each time, not knowing what that meant exactly, but knowing it was bad.

Still, those couple that go well make all the mis-hits worthwhile. Isn't that always the way?

Enjoyment: 7/10
Difficulty: 7/10
Would I do it again? Yes.

86. Go tubing down the Farmington River with my kids

Why you should try it:
Lazing in a tube on a river is the perfect thing for a summer afternoon.

Give it your twist:
- Go snow tubing.
- Try ice fishing.
- Compete at paintballing.

My experience:
The silliness of being stressed out as I rushed somewhere to relax wasn't lost on me, but there I was anyway, feeling my blood pressure rise when we had to run over to an ATM because our place to relax only took cash.

We were in a hurry to fit in tubing down a river after my husband got back late from a morning commitment, and we had an evening thing scheduled for later.

As great as summer vacation is, I am usually guilty of trying to fit in "one more thing" as I see the days before I return to work slipping away.

I had last gone tubing 25 years ago, with the man who would become my husband, on one of our very first dates.

I never forgot that peaceful, easy feeling of floating weightless in the cool water with summer sunshine above me and not a care in the world. In slow sections of the river, I closed my eyes and floated so calmly that I couldn't tell in which direction I was traveling, just a seamless, blissful drift.

I suffer from insomnia occasionally, and one of my best shots for getting back to sleep is to put myself in that tube again, empty my mind, and drift. I can sometimes melt into the mattress and find sweet sleep again.

As pleasing as the tubing was, 25 years went by without a return.

Then I was finally there again, feeling stressed, bickering with my husband, children brought along this time while I tried to squeeze in a bit more summertime fun.

I plopped awkwardly into the tube on the river's edge and felt the water envelop me. It was that perfect temperature, warm enough to be relaxing, cool enough to be refreshing. I started to drift.

Within a few minutes, I was laughing, spinning, holding hands with my husband and my kids, leaning back and closing my eyes without a care in the world.

Bliss.

Enjoyment:	8/10
Difficulty:	3/10
Would I do it again?	Yes.

87. Make a fire in the fireplace

Why you should try it:
Snuggle on a couch in front of a blazing fire; you'll be glad you did.

Give it your twist:
- Start a fire with two sticks.
- Go to a bonfire on a beach.
- Learn how to make five origami animals.

My experience:
See #45: Have dinner by candlelight.

Enjoyment: 5/10
Difficulty: 4/10
Would I do it again? Yes.

88. Give away or throw out my collection of stained glass pieces and scraps

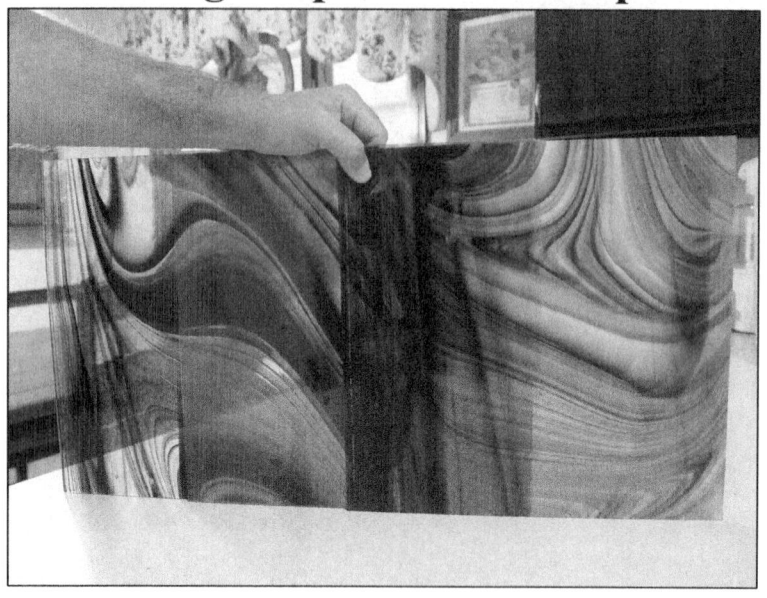

Why you should try it:
Do you have materials from a hobby that you don't use anymore? Finding someone who can use them helps them and clears the clutter, a win-win.

Give it your twist:
- Create a mosaic from broken China pieces.
- Make a decorative stained glass mirror.
- Try glass blowing.

My experience:
I used to make things out of stained glass many years ago (and my dad did many years before me), and I had a big, dangerous box of pieces and scraps in my basement. I finally found a stained glass storeowner who works with children in classroom workshops, and she was glad to put my collection to good use.

Enjoyment:	1/10
Difficulty:	2/10
Would I do it again?	No, that long-neglected chore is done.

89. Adopt a word at savethewords.org

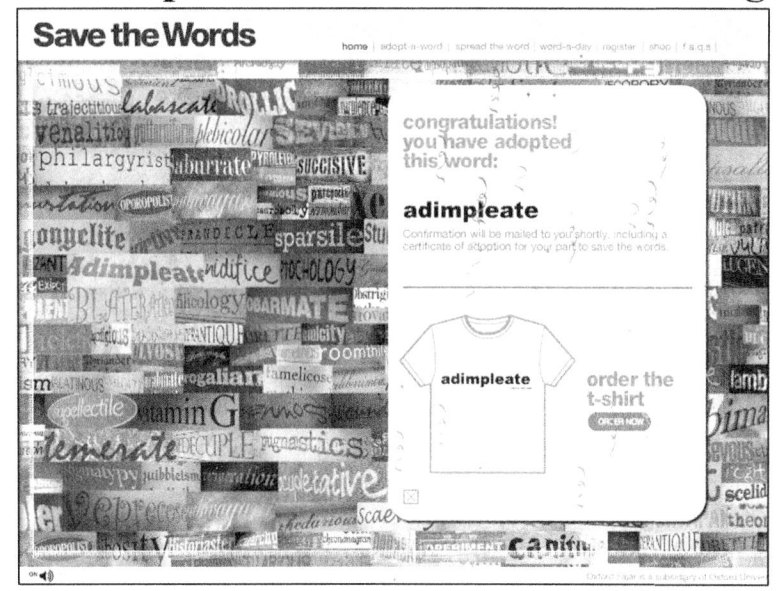

Why you should try it:
Learn a word that is going extinct.
Give it your twist:
- Adopt a rescue animal.
- Say "hello" in 10 languages.
- Learn the alphabet in sign language.

My experience:
During a 6th day off work because of a freak October snowstorm, I found myself with a lot of extra time on my hands. I adopted the word "adimpleate" at savethewords.org, and I was able to adimpleate an unexpected day off with chores that I had been putting off doing.

Enjoyment: 3/10
Difficulty: 1/10
Would I do it again? No.

90. Clean up something outdoors

Why you should try it:
Bring a garbage bag along on a nature walk; it'll be satisfying to clean up an otherwise pretty spot.

Give it your twist:
- Buy a homeless person a meal.
- Go to Burning Man.
- Ride a Segway.

My experience:
There is a group of people who are far from evil, but still hard to understand. They throw their garbage down wherever they happen to be. I live on a fairly busy road, and people will sometimes toss their Burger King trash into my yard as they drive by. They drive along, take the last bite of their Whopper, so clearly it's time to toss their garbage out of their window into my yard.

Do you understand these people?

The other day, I hiked with my family along a stretch of the Metacomet Trail, and we filled up a garbage bag with other people's trash as we went, mostly food wrappers and beer bottles and cans. For the record, slobs who like to dump their garbage in the woods tend to favor Budweiser.

We took a short access trail to a loop trail, and by the time we returned to the access trail, there were two new beer cans laying in wait for us. Busch beer.

We got back to the parking lot and saw a pickup truck with a sloppy bed strewn with garbage. It was sporting a few Busch cans.

I had a passing desire to dump my garbage bag into the bed of their pickup truck. I fought the urge.

It wasn't definite that they were the guilty parties, and that would be wrong, right?

Enjoyment:	6/10
Difficulty:	6/10
Would I do it again?	Yes.

91. Go to a farmer's market

Why you should try it:
Most of the produce and meat in grocery stores is shipped for many miles, reducing freshness and taking an environmental toll. Support the small, local farms in your area.

Give it your twist:
- Stop at a roadside stand for fresh vegetables.
- Research local farms that sell meat and dairy in your town.
- Get a CSA (community supported agriculture) share.

My experience:
From the frizzy headed drunken woman lettuce to the pasture raised multi-colored chicken eggs, Connecticut's bounty beckoned at the Edgewood Park Market in New Haven.

I was stocking up on produce, whole grain breads, and locally raised meats in preparation for a real food mini-pledge. The pledge involves eating whole grains, locally raised meat, and homemade "real" food — food that your great grandmother would have recognized as a girl. If a "food product" is eaten, it should have no more than five ingredients, as a way to cut out a long list of unpronounceable additives.

It was fun to walk around and talk to the farmers about their food. They took obvious pride in their offerings and were happy to answer any questions.

What we purchased:
- 3 whole wheat ciabatta loaves
- 1 baguette
- jar peach ginger jam
- jar raw honey
- 1/2 dozen eggs
- quart sheep's milk yogurt
- lamb and white bean chili
- 1/2 chicken
- 1 lb. beef meatballs
- 1 lb. lamb sausages
- frizzy headed drunken woman lettuce
- 6 tomatoes

We spent about $80. I went and bought some additional groceries from the grocery store, and my food budget for the week wasn't over what I usually spend.

Enjoyment:	5/10
Difficulty:	1/10
Would I do it again?	Yes.

92. Make Spambalaya Jambalaya

Why you should try it:
You probably shouldn't, but it was kind of fun.

Give it your twist:
- Make an old-fashioned Jello salad.
- Cook Coca-Cola cake.
- Google "weird recipes" and knock yourself out.

My experience:
I came across a strange recipe for Spambalaya Jambalaya, and it ended up on my 101 things list. Aside from its awesome name, I had to ask: Why?

Canned spiced meat product mixed with fancy seafood just seemed a little off, and… well, it was.

Pink wine with pink meat
I felt I needed to class things up a bit, so I Googled "What wine do I serve with Spam?" and found this helpful advice:

"I'd look to simple, fruity and accessible reds with SPAM™, seeking the same type of wines that I'd serve with ham: Beaujolais, lighter Pinot Noir, Loire Cabernet Franc or the fruitier sort of Italian reds such as Valpolicella or Bardolino. ... Or rose, of course. After all, the logical extension of the classic rule might be 'pink wine with pink meat.' Finally, don't overlook the possibility that this may just be the time and place to reconsider White Zinfandel. If you're willing to put SPAM™ on your dinner table, why not go the full Monty ... Python?"

A Spam dinner party

I gathered a merry crew to try my Spambalaya Jambalaya with me. After months of trying to get everyone together, it was time to open the cans.

The Spam thudded onto the cutting board with an Alpo-esque *scthfflurumphhh*. We each explored the gelatinous coating and tried the Spam fresh from the can. I knew it would be less than appetizing, but it was grosser than I anticipated, soft, spongy, a sickly pale pink, and salty as hell.

Even though I took on this challenge as a goof, I hardly ever entertain and this was a rare dinner party, so I rued having to put this stuff into my jambalaya.

I cubed it and lightly browned it in olive oil, and it was somewhat improved. Not great, but not going to ruin my dish either. I made my Spambalaya Jambalaya with shrimp, sausage, and Spam, and I served it with mustard greens and cheddar corn bread. And the pink wine, of course.

In the finished dish, the sautéed Spam added bursts of salty silkiness. (How's that for trying to class it up?)

We had a fun meal together and ended on a high note with Alicia's delicious Chocolate Bourbon Pecan Pie.

While the Spam wasn't a total win, at least it reminded me of one of my favorite Monty Python skits.

Enjoyment:	5/10
Difficulty:	7/10
Would I do it again?	No, my poor dinner guests.

93. Go to the beach again

Why you should try it:
Looking out at a distant horizon calms the nerves and recharges the spirit.

Give it your twist:
- Watch sea turtles hatch.
- Make a sandcastle and watch the tide destroy it.
- Ride in a hot air balloon.

My experience:
Somehow the hassle of getting to the beach had kept me from going for years and years. I love it when I'm there, though.

Enjoyment: 7/10
Difficulty: 2/10
Would I do it again? Yes.

94. Eat French fries topped with sweet mango chutney mayo

Why you should try it:
Try a variation on a favorite food.
Give it your twist:
- Try poutine.
- Eat wild blueberries in Maine.
- Have a bite of the smelly fruit durian.

My experience:
During a fun day in New York City, we took a subway down to the East Village and had Belgian fries at Pommes Frites.

There were a large selection of sauces. So many choices! We tried:
- Sweet Mango Chutney Mayo
- Smoked Eggplant Mayo
- Peanut Satay
- Pesto Mayo, and more

The eggplant sauce was my favorite. There are many more sauces to try if we ever make it back.

I'm looking at you, Pomegranate Teriyaki.

Enjoyment:	8/10
Difficulty:	5/10
Would I do it again?	Yes, there's still Pomegranate Teriyaki to try.

95. Fast for one day of Ramadan

Why you should try it:
Fasting will give you an inkling of the sacrifices made by others.
Give it your twist:
- Try a juice cleanse (after checking with a medical professional).
- Take a tour of a mosque.
- Witness a solar eclipse.

My experience:
"There is an unseen sweetness in the stomach's emptiness. We are lutes. When the sound box is filled, no music can come forth."
– Rumi

A cause of lingering guilt: The time I stuffed my face with fragrant fried chicken on the Marrakesh Express in a car shared with a fasting Muslim woman during Ramadan.

That's partly why I gave myself the task to fast for one day of Ramadan. I also wanted to try the fast as an extension of my experience traveling to Morocco, when the end of our trip had coincided with the beginning of Ramadan.

Ramadan is the Muslim holy month, and throughout the month Muslims abstain from food and water from sunrise to sunset, which is one of the Five Pillars of Islam.

Not having water all day was definitely harder than abstaining from food. I stayed indoors in an air-conditioned house, though, so I know my experience was easy compared to that of millions of Muslims who go about their workdays and do it for a month.

My day was uneventful. I stayed up very late the night before and had a meal in the wee hours before sunrise. I slept in and was lethargic throughout the day, the lack of caffeine assuredly having as much impact as the lack of food. I went out to dinner with my husband, waiting until at least 8:19 p.m. to have a drink of water at sunset to break the fast.

I am not religious, but I appreciated getting a small glimpse of the sacrifice of fasting from sunrise to sunset.

Enjoyment: 1/10
Difficulty: 7/10
Would I do it again? No.

96. See at least five live shows

Why you should try it:
Have you stopped going out as much as you used to? Make an effort to get out there. There are always so many things going on, and seeing a live show is exciting.

Give it your twist:
- Go to a comedy club.
- Catch a local play.
- See a magic show.

My experience:
"Ashes of laughter
The ghost is clear
Why do the best things always disappear
Like Ophelia
Please darken my door"
– "Ophelia," The Band

I had the extreme pleasure of attending the Midnight Ramble by one of my favorite musicians, Levon Helm. He was a drummer/singer of The Band, and he performed with his band and many special guests in his home/studio, a big, beautiful barn in the Catskills.

The atmosphere was so warm and welcoming. There were signs asking people to clean up after themselves as this was Levon's home, and it really did have an intimate feel. The stage was on the ground floor of the barn with lofts all around it that allowed fans to look down over the stage.

Levon played the drums for much of the night, singing vocals first on The Band's "Ophelia" in a rollicking version that was adored by the crowd. He came out from his drum kit and performed some songs on mandolin while seated on a stool in center stage.

Several Band songs were featured throughout the night, such as "This Wheel's on Fire," "King Harvest (Has Surely Come)," and "Remedy."

I so enjoyed seeing the love and camaraderie between Levon and the other musicians. The feeling in the room was that these extremely talented people love music and love each other, and the fans that are attracted to the Ramble seemed the same.

I guessed that the final song would be "Up on Cripple Creek," "The Weight," or "I Shall Be Released," and when the opening notes of "The Weight" began, I felt an extreme happiness spread through me. Members of the Steep Canyon Rangers, the opening act, came out for it, with verses being shared all around, some performed on violin, mandolin, and tuba. Levon sang the "Miss Moses" verse.

"Go down, Miss Moses, there's nothing you can say

It's just old Luke, and Luke's waiting on the Judgment Day.

'Well, Luke, my friend, what about young Anna Lee?'

He said, 'Do me a favor, son, won't you stay and keep Anna Lee company?'"

Amy Helm, Levon's daughter, sang several songs and even played drums for a song. Band member Teresa Williams belted out an incredible performance of "Keep Your Lamps Trimmed And Burning."

In their opening set, the Steep Canyon Rangers, a bluegrass group, seemed surprised and thrilled by the enthusiastic response they received. They played with high intensity, their amazing *a cappella* performance of "I Can't Sit Down" being my favorite of the songs they performed.

I also had the opportunity to visit Big Pink, the little house made famous by The Band album, *Music from Big Pink*, one of the greatest albums of all time. It's also the spot where Bob Dylan's *The Basement Tapes* was recorded with The Band.

The house is along a bumpy dirt road with "No Trespassing" signs everywhere, so we snapped a couple quick pictures and were on our way. And I am happy to report that it is still pink.

This was such a delightful trip that any music lover would love. (Update: Levon died about two months after I saw this show.)

Enjoyment: 9/10
Difficulty: 3/10
Would I do it again? Yes to more shows.

97. Make another Shutterfly book

Why you should try it:
Putting your favorite photos from a trip or a holiday into a book is a great way to relive them or share them with others.

Give it your twist:
- Digitize your old family photos.
- Collaborate with relatives on a cookbook of family recipes.
- Make a photo book of your children's best art and schoolwork.

My experience:
Once I went digital, I stopped getting prints of my photos, and I just look at them on my computer. The exception, though, is for trips. I love typing up my travel journal and adding photos from my trip. I've had good experiences with Shutterfly (no affiliation), but there are a lot of other sites where you can do this too.

Enjoyment: 7/10
Difficulty: 3/10
Would I do it again? Yes, I make one for each big trip.

98. Sell some more Elks pins on eBay

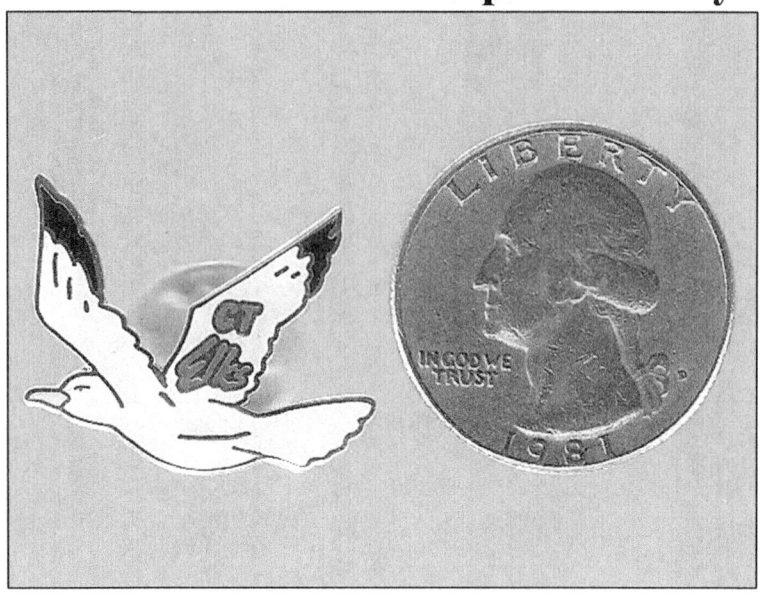

Why you should try it:
Turn your clutter into some cash; chances are that someone in the world wants it.

Give it your twist:
- Wear a brooch you found at a flea market.
- Make a pin out of a foreign coin.
- Donate to a civic organization.

My experience:
My dad had a vast collection of Elks club pins that he collected at Elks conventions over the years. I have set aside some favorites to save, including the ones he designed for the Connecticut Elks, but I have sold a lot of them off, one pin at a time, on eBay. I've made a little pocket change, and I like that they are bringing pleasure to other collectors.

Enjoyment:	2/10
Difficulty:	5/10
Would I do it again?	Yes, someday.

99. Give up caffeine for a day

Why you should try it:

You shouldn't. Coffee is wonderful. But maybe there is something else you would like to give up. Even if you don't want to eliminate something entirely, going without for a while can help you to cut back when you resume having it.

Give it your twist:
- Have no caffeine for a week.
- Go without sugar for a week.
- Give up soda for a month.

My experience:

It took a hurricane to keep me off caffeine for a day.

As Hurricane Irene worked her way up the East coast, I awoke at 6 a.m. without power. I looked at the trees blowing in the wind. With no coffee or Internet calling my name, I fell back asleep. At around 9, we all got up and installed batteries in a portable radio. We heard the news that, yes, there was a hurricane outside and much of the area was without power. We had bowls of cereal with still-cold milk.

I am a coffee fiend, and I was definitely feeling the withdrawal. A low-grade headache and lack of energy were with me most of the day.

I went back to bed and slept until 12:30, as did the rest of my family. I virtually never can fall back asleep once I'm up!

After a lunch of pasta salad that I had prepared the day before, we broke out the board games, which was another item on my list of 101 things.

We all played Monopoly while listening to news updates on the radio.

After a late afternoon update that the storm had passed, we ventured out into the neighborhood for a walk. The rain had stopped, and the wind still gusted occasionally. Some trees were down, and we talked to one neighbor whose roof was damaged, but overall our area was fortunate to not have much damage, although the power was out everywhere.

My sons got hired by a neighbor to do some yard work. While they were down the street, my husband and I started making "Cowboy Chili" over a fire in the backyard. I had some still-frozen ground turkey and homemade chicken stock that I wanted to use up before they went bad, and then I just used whatever else I had on hand.

Cowboy Chili

- 1 lb. ground turkey
- 1 onion, chopped
- 3 cloves garlic, chopped
- canned beans: kidney, pinto, garbanzo
- can diced tomatoes
- 2 cups homemade chicken stock (or water)
- small can green chilies
- small can enchilada sauce
- spice mixture: handful each of cumin, coriander, chili powder; dash each of oregano, salt, and pepper

I usually cook my chili for a long time over low heat. Over the fire, though, it came to a rapid boil and was done in no time. I let it cook for about 10 extra minutes after it was assembled.

It was delicious.

Another item on my "101 things" list was dinner by candlelight. This was not how I initially pictured it, but it was good all the same.

After dinner, we hung out around the radio listening to a show of great stories about nemeses on NPR. I remembered my dad's stories of how excited he was as a boy to wait for "The Shadow" to come on the radio.

We were very fortunate that none of us was hurt, and we had no damage from the storm.

And we had such a great day. It took a hurricane to get us to sleep in, go for a walk together, play a board game, cook over a fire, and gather around the radio. It's hard to imagine a more perfect day spent with my family.

Great as it was, I let out a little squeal of delight when the power came on late the next morning.

Enjoyment: 1/10
Difficulty: 7/10
Would I do it again? Not if I can help it. Keep your hands off my coffee.

100. Have another oyster pan roast at Grand Central Oyster Bar

Why you should try it:
Seek out that perfect dish you had in the past; what one was it?

Give it your twist:
- Try raw oysters.
- Eat a fish you caught yourself.
- Make Eggs Benedict with your own Hollandaise sauce.

My experience:
I love visiting this restaurant right off the train at Grand Central Station. The pan roast is incredibly rich with oysters and cream, definitely a delicacy to enjoy only once in a while.

Enjoyment: 8/10
Difficulty: 1/10
Would I do it again?   Yes.

101. Complete a video game challenge set by my kids

Why you should try it:
Try something that a different generation loves but you just don't get. If you can't beat them, join them.

Give it your twist:
- Go to a heavy metal concert.
- Go speed dating.
- Go ballroom dancing.

My experience:
A noob* gets pwned* (*see glossary)

My two sons and husband were amazed I could even die so early and thought I should get an achieve* just for doing so at level 1. I couldn't help it. I was totally OPed* by the mob* that I attacked. It was my first time trying an MMORPG*, and my first PvE* went horribly wrong. But at least I got a green* a little bit later.

Let me back up a bit. I agreed to try World of Warcraft for two hours to complete a task on my 101 things list. The timing could have been better, as my two teenage boys had picked up the habit of talking about WoW in esoteric jargon at all hours of the day and night.

I played as a female Troll Warrior named MartyrSauce of the Quel'dore realm.

My two hours didn't go well. My son David sat beside me to help. He really tried his hardest to be patient, but his instructions were littered with statements like these:
- No, Mom, that's a cactus.
- Mom, there's a way up the hill.
- No, Mom, you need to go *through* the door.
- You're invincible, Mom, which is a good thing.
- Mom, you're still fighting.

I'm afraid to say that it wasn't a very fun experience for either me or my son, who periodically grabbed the mouse from me and starting clicking away in frustration. I ended up reaching level 6. My son had thought I would be able to get to level 15 in the time frame.

In my defense, Pac-Man never made me drop totems while in combat with scorpions to collect their venom.

*Glossary

- noob – newbie; someone inexperienced in the game, often stupidly so
- pwned – defeated; "owned"
- achieve – achievement; one of the many, many shortened words
- OPed – overpowered
- mob – short for mobile; enemy
- MMORPG – massively multiplayer online role-playing game
- PvE – player versus environment
- green – an item with stats, or that gives extra bonuses; their names are green in the game

Enjoyment: 1/10
Difficulty: 9/10
Would I do it again? No, please no.

On completing 101 things in 1001 days

> Most of the things you'll do "someday" won't happen on their own. If you want to fly on a trapeze, you have to get to that class, and you have to climb that ladder.

I completed 101 things in 1001 days, a quest that took a lot of my energy for two and three-quarter years, but gave back more than it took.

My list took me to Manhattan for a flying trapeze, Philly for a cheesesteak, Costa Rica on my own. I drank cow's milk straight from a teat, got a (fake) bottle smashed over my head, jumped off a cliff. I saw the sun rise over Machu Picchu and set 12 hours later on the road back to Cuzco. I ran a Rugged Maniac, made my first soufflé, did 50 consecutive push-ups, said yes to everything, and sent my poo off in the mail.

My friends joined me to ride a mechanical bull, paint a nude model, and fire a gun. They got me up a tree. My husband drove me six hours so I could take a 30-second zorbing ride, flew on that trapeze himself, and taught me how to use a chop saw. My kids ate freshly baked bread, picked out random dinner ingredients, and cleaned up a hiking trail.

In any given week, I would be memorizing a 131-line poem, practicing juggling, trying to stay awake through *Das Boot*, looking up where I could go snowboarding, and inventing a recipe for vegan cake pops.

I dusted off my old guitar and tried out my unplayed bodhrán too. I brewed my own beer and served dinner party guests Spambalaya. I became a zombie for a day and had little fish nibble my toes. I visited museums with bad art and good sex. I ate haggis and toured my state for hot dogs. I sprayed graffiti on my garage.

I tried out Zumba and haiku and World of Warcraft, was bad at all and didn't care (too much). I hiked Mount Katahdin and had cartoons try to teach me to dance. I fasted for Ramadan, attended a UU sermon, and cooked at a soup kitchen.

There were plenty of items that weren't so fun. I finalized my will, cleaned out my closets, gave away old board games. I did those chores that would be done "someday" — or probably never. I walked and walked, sometimes in circles. I stopped complaining and started knitting. I grew tomatoes.

Most of all, I became less timid and squeamish, and I don't feel that fearful insecurity about new things the way I used to.

I've been struck by the number of people who've said about even mundane things that they've always wanted to try that, whether it was making pasta, going tubing, or listening to records that were boxed up for 20 years.

I am introverted with no special talents, but I feel a new confidence, and I marvel at the excitement around every corner. I don't believe in blessings, but I know that I am blessed, and I thank the universe and my family and friends for giving me an interesting life.

Life is full of special moments, and instead of letting your ideas of things you'd like to do flit through your mind and disappear with a wistful "someday," get out there and do them.

Most of the things you'll do "someday" won't happen on their own. If you want to fly on a trapeze, you have to get to that class, and you have to climb that ladder.

I would love to hear from you if you try any of these challenges or make a list of your own: marcy@tootimidandsqueamish.com

Or visit my blog and leave a comment: tootimidandsqueamish.com

Let me know, too, of any new challenges you think I should try.

Celebrate your courage by sending me a handmade postcard about how you have broken out of your comfort zone, and I may feature it on my blog. More information: http://www.tootimidandsqueamish.com/send-me-your-postcard/

Finally, please consider reviewing this book on Amazon.com.
